Hidden History
of Civil War
Savannah

Michael L. Jordan

Foreword by Jim Morekis

THE
History
PRESS

Published by The History Press
Charleston, SC
www.historypress.net

Front cover, top left: Library of Congress; *top center*: bequest of Robert E. Lee , III, Washington and Lee University, Lexington, Virginia; *top right*: author's collection; *bottom*: estate of Judy L. Wood. *Back cover*: Library of Congress.

First published 2017

Manufactured in the United States

ISBN 9781626196438

Library of Congress Control Number: 2016961744

Notice: The information in this book is true and complete to the best of our knowledge. It is offered without guarantee on the part of the author or The History Press. The author and The History Press disclaim all liability in connection with the use of this book.

To my parents, Marjorie and Morris

CONTENTS

FOREWORD

It seems that no matter what else might change in America, our collective fascination with the Civil War remains unbroken.

Whether because the country still wrestles with so many of its ancillary issues today, or because of its stirring and very human tales of courage, or because of the way Americans reconciled after our bloodiest conflict—or because of all three—the events of 1861–65 resonate with us a century and a half after the war's end.

While Savannah, Georgia, is very much in touch with its colonial and Revolutionary War past, the Civil War left its mark here as well—not in fire and ember, as in Atlanta or in Columbia, South Carolina, but in affirming Savannah's identity as a bit more individualistic, a bit truer to itself, a bit off the beaten path, even for Southern cities.

Michael Jordan's new book, *Hidden History of Civil War Savannah*, delivers more than the promise of its title. In my years of familiarity with his passion for history and dedication to scholarship, I've also learned that Michael has one of the rarest of scholarly gifts: he communicates that passion for history with skill, humor, confidence and real accessibility.

Whether in his written projects or in his many fine independent video productions—which have set the regional standard—Michael has always reached for more than the mundane.

Even a glance at the chapter titles of *Hidden History* shows that this is no regurgitation of things you already know. You'll find tales of soldierly bravery, for sure. But you'll also read about the largely forgotten, controversial

"Corner-stone Speech," delivered in Savannah by Alexander Stephens, which made stark the South's morally indefensible reason for secession.

You'll also read lesser-known facts about very well-known people, such as the young Robert E. Lee. As a U.S. Army officer, he helped build the same Fort Pulaski that would be one of the Union's earliest prizes of war when it was recaptured from its Confederate garrison.

Savannah has its share of tour guides. I'm chagrined to say that some of them are, shall we say, occasionally tempted to embellish the truth a bit.

Like myself, Michael has a journalism background. He knows the value of accuracy, of authenticity, of first-person experience. *Hidden History of Civil War Savannah* exemplifies all three.

I've written several travel guidebooks, and as I write them, I always keep Michael's example in mind: take care of the truth, and the fun will follow.

The old line goes that truth is stranger than fiction. As any journalist, historian and history buff knows, however, truth is also usually much more interesting than fiction.

There's no need to embellish a history as grand and intriguing as Savannah's, anyway.

JIM MOREKIS
Author and editor-in-chief of *Connect Savannah* magazine

ACKNOWLEDGEMENTS

The genesis of this book was a January 2013 conversation with eminent Savannah educator and historian Dr. Paul M. Pressly, who convinced me that I had the knowledge and skill to write in depth about Savannah's history. Hugh Golson, descendant of so many noteworthy Savannahians of long ago and keeper of countless stories, read virtually everything I wrote and offered insight at every turn. Hugh also shared his extensive and ever-growing personal collection of period images of Savannah. The incomparable Dr. Maurice "Mel" Melton, author of *The Best Station of Them All: The Savannah Squadron, 1861–1865*, kept me straightened out during my feeble attempt to dabble in his waters of Civil War naval history when I wrote about the ill-fated CSS *Atlanta*. Lieutenant Colonel Henry W. Persons Jr. and National Park Service historian Jim Burgess of Manassas National Battlefield Park were immeasurably helpful as I wrote about Francis S. Bartow and the Oglethorpe Light Infantry at the Battle of First Manassas.

Mazie Bowen, public service coordinator at the University of Georgia's Special Collections Library, was always available with a quick scan of a source document or an image. The archivists at the Georgia Historical Society's Research Center, the Louis Round Wilson Special Collections Library at the University of North Carolina at Chapel Hill and the David M. Rubenstein Rare Book & Manuscript Library at Duke University were instrumental as well. The folks at Washington & Lee University bent over backward to help me obtain a portrait of young U.S. Army lieutenant

Robert E. Lee in time to meet my deadline. Luciana Spracher, director of the City of Savannah Research Library and Municipal Archives, was as much a partner in this project as she has been in so many of my historical documentaries over the years.

Jeff Seymour, director of education and history at the National Civil War Naval Museum in Columbus, Georgia, was tremendously helpful with access to typescripts of period diaries. Reference librarian Sharen Lee at the Bull Street Library in Savannah continued her tradition of going out of her way to help me find what I needed. Kelly Westfield, a graduate student in public history at my alma mater, Armstrong State University in Savannah, rendered invaluable service locating and copying historic newspaper articles and primary sources at libraries and archives in Savannah.

Mick McCay ran around downtown Savannah in the aftermath of Hurricane Matthew to get me the correct punctuation for the text on the Confederate Monument. Fenton Martin and Dr. Christopher Hendricks helped me clean up and correctly organize more than four hundred endnotes and my bibliography.

My mother-in-law, Margarete Neate, worked as a full-time child-care provider for a month to enable me to write the first few chapters of this work. My wife (and published author), Dr. Krista Wiegand, graciously shouldered many of my usual tasks and responsibilities so that I could devote the time and energy required to finish the book. She offered wise counsel, endured my long-winded stories and tempered my perfectionism. I could ask for no greater partner or friend. Finally, this project has spanned more than half the life of my son Joseph, who has found his own unique and endearing ways to support his daddy's book.

SAVANNAH

More than Just a City That Sherman Didn't Burn

Walk down one of Savannah's tree-shaded downtown streets on any given day and you're likely to hear the voice of a tour guide wafting on the breeze behind a passing trolley or echoing off the thick trunks of the live oak trees and the brick walls of the historic houses. "General William T. Sherman's 'March to the Sea' ended here in Savannah in December 1864." The guide will inform his or her guests—correctly—that Savannah mayor Richard Arnold and a small group of aldermen rode out to meet Sherman's advancing army outside the city limits in order to surrender the defenseless city, that Sherman lodged in the stately Green-Meldrim House on Madison Square and proceeded, in a telegram, to present Savannah to President Abraham Lincoln as "a Christmas gift," complete with thousands of bales of cotton.

While the story is true, and truly fascinating, it barely scratches the surface of this historic city's rich and fascinating experience in the American Civil War. Here, in Savannah, the Confederacy's vice president declared to the world that slavery was the "corner-stone" of the new Southern republic. Here a brash politician-turned-soldier defied Georgia's governor and marched off to die, alongside six of his young troops, in the first battle of the war. On a meandering saltwater creek just outside town, a menacing "iron monster" steamed out to do battle with two of the North's most fearsome ironclad warships. Savannah was twice the temporary home of the South's most famous general, Robert E. Lee, who presided over the redesign of the area's coastal fortifications before he assumed command in Virginia and became a legend. Here, on the edge of a sprawling, green park where thousands of locals and tourists enjoy concerts, picnics and farmer's markets, more than five thousand pitiful Union prisoners were once packed into a rough wooden stockade. In the days before an imposing steel and concrete span first conveyed motorists from Savannah to South Carolina, ten thousand bedraggled Confederate soldiers made the crossing on a temporary floating bridge cobbled together from rickety wooden barges. Incredibly, just days after Sherman captured Savannah, a majority of the city's leading citizens voted not just to surrender, but to rejoin the Union, turning their backs on their sons and husbands fighting in Confederate armies on other battlefields. Here, weeks after Savannah's war ended, the city did burn in a spectacular, explosive fire, with some loss of life and great damage to property. And now, more than a century and a half after these events took place, a bronze statue of a Confederate soldier stands sentinel over the scene, while a marble figure titled *Silence* lifts a finger to her lips as she surveys the graves of more than seven hundred Confederate soldiers.

Truly, Savannah is a Civil War city, an epicenter of activity in the conflict that southerners like to call "the War Between the States." Far from being just a place that Sherman chose not to burn or, in the words of the great local historian Alexander Lawrence, "A Present for Mr. Lincoln," Savannah is a gift for anyone who loves a good story about our nation's past.

1

WHAT'S IT REALLY ALL ABOUT?

Alexander Stephens and His "Corner-stone Speech" in Savannah, March 1861

Our new government is founded upon exactly the opposite idea; its foundations are laid, its corner-stone rests upon the great truth, that the negro is not equal to the white man; that slavery—subordination to the superior race—is his natural and normal condition.
—Confederate vice president Alexander Stephens in Savannah, March 21, 1861

Today, tourists stroll through Savannah's Chippewa Square blissfully unaware of its noteworthy association with one of the South's darkest Civil War secrets. Many disobey warning signs and step onto the brick base of Daniel Chester French's 1910 statue of Georgia founder James Oglethorpe. Others amble about beneath the shade of the spreading live oak trees, searching for the bench where Tom Hanks's character in the 1994 movie *Forrest Gump* famously intoned, "Mama always said life was like a box of chocolates. You never know what you're gonna get."

Some may be aware that Forrest Gump's namesake was Confederate general Nathan Bedford Forrest, leader of the Ku Klux Klan. It's less likely that anyone save a few history-minded locals will remember that the two busts of Confederate generals currently located in the center of Savannah's Forsyth Park once stood here in the center of the square, before they were moved to make way for Oglethorpe. But these are mere hints of the true secret in question. It is hidden in the history of the Art Moderne theater perched on the northeast trust lot on the eastern edge of the square. (Trust lots are large parcels situated, two per side, on the eastern and western sides

The Savannah Theatre as it appeared in the nineteenth century. *Georgia Historical Society.*

of each of Savannah's twenty-two historic downtown squares. Part of James Oglethorpe's unique city design, trust lots are typically set aside for large public buildings or mansions).

This building, the Savannah Theatre, is in some senses one of the oldest structures in the city. British architect William Jay, who is also responsible for such Savannah landmarks as the Owens-Thomas House on Oglethorpe Square, the Telfair mansion (now the Telfair Academy of Art) on Telfair Square and the Scarborough mansion on West Broad Street (now the Ships of the Sea Maritime Museum), designed the first theater building here in 1818. Jay's structure burned down in 1906, and the rebuilt structure was charred again in 1948, though portions of the original north and east walls remain, concealed beneath the modern stucco. Today's iteration features an exuberantly flashing neon "Savannah" sign, a cylindrical glass ticket booth and a wide marquee. The exterior stairs climbing up the south face of the structure—a holdover from days when black theatergoers were required to use a separate entrance—usually go unnoticed, though they are a legacy of the racial bias that was once preached on this very spot by a leading Confederate politician.[1]

On the evening of Thursday, March 21, 1861, the dusty square outside the theater, which was then called the Athenaeum, was thronged with people from all over Georgia. The state secession convention was meeting in the city—not to officially bring Georgia out of the Union, which had been accomplished two months earlier during a previous session in the state capital of Milledgeville—but rather to ratify the national Constitution of the Confederate States of America and fashion a new state constitution to reflect its principles. Because of this gathering, the city was full of important visitors.[2] Local newspapers had advertised that one of the new republic's leading voices, Alexander Stephens, the provisional vice president of the

Confederacy, would give a public address at the Athenaeum. In an age before television, radio or movies, and in a time when political change was gripping people of all classes, Stephens's appearance was the biggest draw of the season.

Stephens was scheduled to begin speaking at 7:30 p.m., but the Athenaeum was standing room–only long before the appointed hour. "The crowd in the building could not have numbered less than two thousand," proclaimed the *Savannah Republican* of March 22, 1861, "for every square foot of it was packed, from pit to dome." The first tier of seats was reserved for ladies, but many women were forced to find spots to stand among men on the third floor and elsewhere. Even the stage was crowded with seats claimed by important visitors in town for the secession convention. The *Savannah Daily Morning News* reported on March 22 that many attendees were simply unable to bear the crush of people. "Indeed, so crowded was the house," wrote a correspondent, "that many ladies and gentlemen, who were unable to stand the pressure, with much difficulty regained the street, where they joined the immense throng of outsiders."

When those fortunate enough to retain their seats, or spots, within the theater caught their first glimpse of Alexander Stephens, it is possible some were shocked by his appearance. Frail, pasty and emaciated, this former Georgia congressman looked like a sick little boy, even though he stood a respectable five feet, seven inches tall—not much shorter than the average American man of his day. According to Stephens's biographer Thomas E. Schott:

> *He looked like a freak. His head was small, with protruding, slightly oversized ears. A pair of blazing black eyes, wide-set on either side of a thin, sharp nose, dominated his ashen countenance. Thin, pale lips turned downward at the corners. His long, bony fingers looked like claws attached to the ends of broomstick arms.*[3]

Alexander Hamilton Stephens, Confederate vice president and postwar governor of Georgia. *National Archives.*

Mayor Charles C. Jones Jr. waited for the "deafening rounds of applause" to subside before introducing Stephens.

The vice president began to speak, but he had barely completed his opening pleasantries when he was interrupted by a ruckus outside the auditorium. Angry Savannahians were demanding that Stephens step out of the building to deliver his remarks, since more people were waiting outside the Athenaeum than within. Mayor Jones silenced the crowd by explaining that Stephens's health would not permit him to speak in the open air. Stephens countered that he would speak in the location that was best for the ladies who were present. "There was a general cry indoors" to the effect that the ladies could not bear to be outdoors, so Stephens announced that he would remain where he was. Not surprisingly, this outcome did not sit well with the multitude outside, which erupted into what one eyewitness described as an "uproar and clamor." They demanded speeches from *someone*, and a few of the dignitaries in the hall stepped out to oblige them with short, extemporaneous addresses. Eventually, after learning that Governor Joseph E. Brown and Confederate secretary of state Robert Toombs had arrived in Savannah, some of the crowd migrated to the Pulaski House hotel on Johnson Square, where the men were lodging, to demand a speech from them. Never before and perhaps never since has Savannah been plagued by a roving band of citizens angrily demanding an oration.[4]

Through it all, Stephens waited patiently. "So great was the confusion," wrote the *Republican*, "it was a long time before he could proceed with his speech."[5] Scolding his audience like a patient schoolteacher, a profession which he briefly practiced before beginning his career in politics, Stephens chided, "When perfect quiet is restored, I shall proceed. I cannot speak so long as there is any noise or confusion. I shall take my time. I feel quite prepared to spend the night with you if necessary." As it turned out, Stephens would captivate his audience for close to two hours—long enough to make history.[6]

Stephens began innocuously enough, bragging about the fact that Confederate independence, which he described as "one of the greatest revolutions in the annals of the world," had been achieved without any shedding of blood up to that point. (The first shots of the war, fired on Fort Sumter in Charleston Harbor, were still three weeks away.) He proceeded to delineate similarities and differences between the United States Constitution and the new Confederate States Constitution. The latter, he claimed, improved upon the original by, among other things, prescribing a longer, six-year term for the president and vice president. Stephens touched briefly on questions of taxation, regional interests and the powers of the new (Southern) federal government. Then Stephens abruptly stopped his humdrum soliloquy and tossed his audience a large portion of political red meat. "The new constitution has put at rest, forever," he declared, "all the agitating questions relating to our peculiar institution, African slavery."[7]

Slavery, Stephens judged, "was the immediate cause" of Southern secession and the establishment of the Confederate States. The seeds of the Southern revolution had been sown—inadvertently—by Thomas Jefferson, the author of the Declaration of Independence, when he famously wrote in that founding document, "all men are created equal." Stephens explained that Jefferson and most of his fellow founding fathers believed that "the enslavement of the African was in violation of the laws of nature; that it was wrong in principle, socially, morally, and politically." The founders did not know how to confront the evil in their day, but were certain that one day in the not too distant future, slavery would end on its own. "Those ideas," however, "were fundamentally wrong," Stephens insisted. "They rested upon the assumption of the equality of races. This was an error." Alluding to the biblical parable of the wise man who built his house on a rock, allowing it to withstand the trials of life, Stephens branded the concept of racial equality "a sandy foundation," and argued that "the government built upon it [the U.S. government pre-secession] fell when the 'storm came and the wind blew.'" With the stage set—the battlefield prepared—Stephens unleashed his most revolutionary and, to modern readers upsetting, contention:

> *Our new government is founded upon exactly the opposite idea; its foundations are laid, its corner-stone rests upon the great truth, that the negro is not equal to the white man; that slavery—subordination to the superior race—is his natural and normal condition. This, our new government, is the first, in the history of the world, based upon this great physical, philosophical, and moral truth.*

Abolitionists were, in Stephens's view, "fanatics," who "were attempting to make things equal which the Creator had made unequal." All white people, declared Stephens, "however high or low, rich or poor, are equal in the eye of the law. Not so with the negro. Subordination is his place. He, by nature, or by the curse against Canaan, is fitted for that condition which he occupies in our system."[8]

While shocking and terribly offensive to most Americans today, the ideas about race that Stephens enunciated were, to one extent or another, commonly held by Southerners and even many Northerners at the time and would not have been upsetting to his audience. What makes Stephens's

March 21, 1861 address in Savannah so remarkable is not the assertions it makes about the place of the African American in society, but rather the fact that Stephens announced to the world that keeping the black man in his place was the main focus of the Confederate constitution, and therefore of the entire Confederate nation. Here is the zinger that gives Stephens's entire speech the name by which it has been known for more than 150 years:

> *Our confederacy is founded upon principles in strict conformity with these laws. This stone which was rejected by the first builders "is become the chief of the corner"—the real "corner-stone"—in our new edifice.*

Here Stephens is once again making a direct reference to a scripture that would have been familiar to his Christian listeners: Psalms 118:22, in which the Psalmist declares, "The stone which the builders rejected has become the chief corner stone." King David is considered the original author of the text, though Jesus quoted the verse at the end of a parable that is included in three of the four New Testament Gospels. In Stephens's allegory, slavery, the "peculiar institution" that so vexed the founders as they framed the Constitution and cobbled together a new nation in 1776, had broken that nation apart and simultaneously become the basis of a new one. Simply put, Stephens was declaring African slavery to be more than an economic system or even a way of life; slavery and white supremacy were the very foundations upon which the entire structure of the Confederate States of America was built.

To the breathless throng jammed into the stifling Athenaeum, "Stephens' words were gospel," wrote biographer Schott. This gospel, if it can be called that, fell from the lips of its giver completely unscripted, for Stephens confirmed after the war that he spoke extemporaneously in Savannah. The only written text of the address was created by a *Savannah Republican* reporter who was in the audience. Stephens himself checked over the rough transcription before its publication, yet complained later that his words were printed "with several glaring errors."[9] Still, though he argued in later years that too much importance was placed on his statements about slavery as the cause of secession (that passage comprised just 28 percent of the 4,843 words in the *Savannah Republican* text of the speech), Stephens never reversed himself on the question of whether blacks were inherently inferior to whites or whether slavery was the natural condition of African Americans. Just one month later, in a speech before the Virginia secession convention in Richmond, Stephens repeated the theme, asserting: "As a race, the African is inferior to the white man. Subordination to the white man is his normal condition. He is not his equal by nature, and cannot be made so by human laws or human institutions."[10] And even when the cause was lost and he was a prisoner in Boston Harbor in 1865, Stephens maintained, "The order of subordination was nature's great law; philosophy taught that order as the normal condition of the African amongst European races."[11]

Stephens's brash declaration in Savannah on March 21, 1861, has taken on great importance in the ensuing century and a half, especially when it comes to ascertaining the real cause of the American Civil War. The vice president's words are taken as clear proof that the Confederate cause was racist to the core and that Southerners fought primarily to keep their slaves. Conversely, Confederate apologists point out that Stephens's proslavery rhetoric appears nowhere in speeches by other Confederate leaders, whose proclamations and pronouncements focused primarily on states' rights—the right of states to supersede the power of the federal government—and other regional differences as the root causes of the conflict.[12] We can only assume that Stephens meant what he said.

Stephens returned to Savannah just over two decades later, freed from postwar prison, rehabilitated and serving as Georgia's elected governor. He was to speak on the 150th anniversary of the founding of Georgia as a British colony in February 1733. An overnight train ride and an early-morning arrival weakened the immune system of this already frail politician, and the carriage that carried Stephens from the train station to his hotel had a broken window, allowing the bitterly cold air to enter the vehicle. A few days after his return to Milledgeville, Governor Stephens fell ill. He slipped into eternity on March 4, 1883. The same city that had cemented Stephens's place as a cornerstone of the Southern Confederacy had become the scene of the closing act of his political life.[13]

FRANCIS S. BARTOW

Savannah's Confederate Martyr

They have killed me, but, boys, NEVER give up the field.
—last words of Colonel Francis S. Bartow, as quoted in the
Savannah Daily Morning News, *August 1, 1861*

Perhaps no other individual is more responsible for Georgia leaving the Union than Francis S. Bartow. This Savannah attorney, orator and military commander helped plunge his city and state headlong into war, losing his life in the first battle of the conflict. Bartow's words and deeds lifted him to the heights of Confederate immortality. Bartow was the subject of the war's first battlefield monument and the recipient of numerous tributes in the twentieth century. Today, however, his story is all but forgotten.

Francis Stebbins Bartow was born on September 6, 1816, in Savannah, the son of local physician Theodosius Bartow and the former Frances Lloyd Stebbins.[14] Bartow wed Louisa G. Berrien in Chatham County on April 18, 1844—the sixty-eighth year, the marriage certificate proudly proclaims, of the independence of the United States.[15] Perhaps in hindsight this attestation presaged Bartow's death in the service of another aspiring young republic. At some point, Bartow and his bride took up residence in Theodosius's imposing mansion at the corner of Harris and Barnard Streets on Pulaski Square.[16] The union brought Bartow into one of the South's most politically prominent families, for Louisa was the eighth of sixteen children born to John Macpherson Berrien, a lawyer, judge, two-time U.S. senator and attorney general in Andrew Jackson's first administration.

John Berrien was also a wealthy Savannah planter who owned more than 140 slaves.[17]

After graduating from the University of Georgia with highest honors in 1835, Francis Bartow attended Yale Law School for a time and returned to Savannah to practice law without having earned a degree.[18] He joined his father-in-law's law firm and was soon elected to state office, serving two terms in the Georgia House of Representatives and one term in the state senate.[19] Bartow, a leading member of the Whig Party, was considered to be a persuasive politician. A Savannah newspaper opined, "by the logical force and clearness of his argument, as well as by the power of his eloquence, he greatly and at once distinguished himself, thus early giving assurance of the high position which he afterwards attained by his profession."[20]

Francis S. Bartow, an impassioned orator who won his battle with Georgia's governor but lost his life in the first battle of the war. *Georgia Historical Society.*

In 1857, Bartow was elected to the recently vacated captaincy of a newly formed Savannah militia unit known as the Oglethorpe Light Infantry—the "Oglethorpes," for short—one of many such armed organizations in the city. Unlike other storied local units, such as the Chatham Artillery, which traces its origins to a British colonial militia unit organized in 1751, and the Savannah Volunteer Guards, which participated in the War of 1812, the Oglethorpes were a new group of young aristocrats, organized on January 8, 1856. Bartow was just their second captain.[21] According to an apocryphal story, Bartow had a singular method for testing the bravery and courage of recruits: he flicked water on the young men's faces; if the water sizzled, the soldier was acceptable. Reportedly, someone asked, "How many have you sent home so far?" Bartow is said to have replied, "None—so far. They always sizzle."[22]

In spite of his connections and early accomplishments, the young Bartow might have toiled in relative obscurity were it not for the rise of a movement clamoring for the secession of the slave-holding Southern states. Bartow, a gifted orator, put his skills to frequent and effective use in support of the cause. According to the *Savannah Daily Morning News*, "His style of oratory was bold, earnest and impassioned. As a determined advocate, his eloquence was of a high and thrilling order."[23] At the Masonic Hall in Savannah on September 17, 1860, Bartow declared:

> *I am tired of this endless controversy. I am wearied with seeing this threatening cloud forever above our heads. If the storm is to come, and it seems to me as though it must, be its fury ever so great, I court it now in the day of my vigor and strength....Let it come now, I am ready for it....I do not wish to destroy this Government. I am a Union man in every fibre [sic] of my heart...but I will peril all—ALL before I will abandon our rights in the Union or submit to be governed by an unprincipled majority.*[24]

Speaking three months later at a secession rally in Atlanta, Bartow was handed a note informing him of the Federal destruction of Fort Moultrie in Charleston Harbor—a prelude to the bombardment of Fort Sumter the following April. "Is this gallant, noble state of South Carolina, that had the boldness to take the lead in this matter, to be left to the cold calculating of the cooperationists of Georgia?" he cried. "No! Never!" the crowd roared in reply. Then, with a tone described by an eyewitness as "biting sarcasm," Bartow leveled a charge: "while you *talk* of *cooperation*, you hear the thunders [*sic*] of the cannon, and the clash of the sabres reach you from South Carolina."[25] Georgia's honor was on the line, and Bartow was making it clear where he believed the state's loyalties should lie. The young firebrand put the force of arms behind his words on January 3, 1861, when, acting on orders from Georgia governor Joseph E. Brown, Bartow helped lead a force of local Georgia state troops to seize Federal-held Fort Pulaski near the mouth of the Savannah River.[26]

As the Southern states marched steadily toward disunion, the citizens of Chatham County sent Bartow to be one of their three representatives at the Georgia secession convention in Milledgeville. In January 1861, all three men signed Georgia's Ordinance of Secession, voting with the majority in favor of leaving the Union.[27] In February, Bartow was chosen to represent Georgia in the unicameral Provisional Congress of the Confederate States, meeting in Montgomery, Alabama. He was placed at the head of the influential military affairs committee at a time when the young Southern republic was making its first preparations for war. During his tenure, some historians contend, Bartow placed an enduring stamp on Confederate military history when he suggested gray as the color for Confederate uniforms. The seed was planted, the story goes, when Bartow was impressed with the new coarse gray uniforms adopted by the Savannah Volunteer Guards. Former Guards commander William Starr Basinger wrote in his memoirs, "Captain Bartow…told the writer that it was himself who insisted on the adoption of gray as the color of the uniform prescribed for the Army of the Confederate States; and that he did so because he had seen and admired so much the gray service uniform of the Guards."[28] The author has located no other sources for the story and indeed found competing claims about the true origins of Confederate gray.

Regardless of the role he played in designing the Confederacy's military uniform, it is clear that Bartow was anxious to don it in defense of his new nation. Patriotic young men in every Southern city heard the drumbeat of war calling them to Virginia, where it became more obvious every day that Union and Confederate forces would soon do battle. Savannah was caught up in the fervor. One young Savannahian, Lieutenant George Anderson Mercer, wrote in his diary on April 25, 1861, "Many of our men are burning to fly to the assistance of old Virginia."[29] Before Bartow and his men could cross swords with the enemy in Virginia, they would first have to win a battle of wills with Governor Brown, a staunch states' rights advocate who repeatedly insisted that state troops should remain within Georgia's borders and under his command. Brown stubbornly refused to give his consent for the Oglethorpes to depart for Virginia.

Conveniently, Bartow's colleagues in the Provisional Confederate Congress provided a loophole. On May 10, 1861, the congress passed an act authorizing Confederate president Jefferson Davis to personally accept the services of individual military units whose members were willing to enlist for the duration of the war. Until that time, Confederate units enlisted only for set periods, ranging from six months to a year.[30] As soon as the act was passed, Bartow rushed to the telegraph office in Montgomery and sent a message to Savannah, informing the Oglethorpes of the good news. The telegram was received around 4:00 p.m., and officers sent word for the members of the unit to gather that evening at the Oglethorpe Barracks on Madison Square—where the Hilton Savannah DeSoto is located today. After an officer read Bartow's message aloud, the soldiers voted unanimously to offer their services to President Davis. The men telegraphed their intentions to Bartow, who delivered the news in person to the president. According to a newspaper correspondent, "This company was the first one to offer its services to President Davis under the Confederate act authorizing him to

Governor Joseph E. Brown waged a bitter war of words with Francis Bartow in a vain attempt to keep the Oglethorpe Light Infantry from leaving the state. *Library of Congress.*

receive independent companies, and had the honor of being the first received....They have enlisted for the whole war, and not one will turn back who can go forward, until it is ended, or they are completely annihilated."[31] These words would prove prophetic.

Bartow rushed home from Montgomery on the evening of Sunday, May 19. At 12:30 p.m. on Tuesday, May 21, the men gathered once again at the Oglethorpe Barracks, where Major Montgomery Gardner, who would later rise to the rank of brigadier general, mustered ninety-seven men and four commissioned officers into the Confederate army. The average age of the soldiers was nineteen years old, though several were younger.[32]

Duly sworn in, the troops formed up at 12:30 p.m. on the Oglethorpes' parade ground at the intersection of South Broad (modern-day Oglethorpe Avenue) and Bull Streets. Accompanied by other Savannah militia units, Bartow's troops marched west to Whitaker Street as drumbeats and the strains of William Dressler's 1854 tune "Bold Soldier Boy" filled the air.[33] The formation stopped at the home of Thomas Holcombe at the northwest corner of Whitaker and Gaston Streets, where the Oglethorpes were presented a silk First Confederate National Flag, known as the "Stars and Bars," sewn and donated by a group of local ladies. Attorney Frederick Tupper, speaking on the women's behalf, addressed the assembled soldiers:

They give it [the flag] *to you in the confidence that in your keeping it will suffer no disgrace; that you will guard it as your honor—if need be, with your lives....And when the fight is over, and peace, sweet peace, has settled dovelike on our land, that you will return with it—battered and torn it may be, begrimed with the smoke of battle—but glorious with the halo of victory around it.*

Touching on a subject that would become the source of great friction between Bartow and Georgia's governor, Tupper continued: "True you leave your home, but it matters very little whether you fought here or there—a blow struck for Virginia is a blow for Georgia. For are not Virginia and Georgia now united? Have they not one cause, one hope, one destiny?" Bartow responded, extemporaneously, that "if it [the flag] was not brought back emblazoned with glory, it would be because there was not an arm left to strike the blow."[34] One eyewitness reported that the scene stirred up deep feelings among onlookers, and "tears coursed down many a rugged cheek."[35]

Onlookers showered the departing soldiers with flowers as they marched north to Liberty Street, then west to the Central of Georgia Railroad depot on West Broad Street. Here they bade farewell to friends and family and climbed aboard Charleston and Savannah Railroad cars to begin their journey to Virginia. The train, scheduled to leave at 1:45 p.m., delayed its departure by half an hour to accommodate the troops.[36] The *Savannah Republican* reported that, "as the train moved off an immense shout went up from the vast multitude, while hats, handkerchiefs and everything available was waiving [sic] in the air."[37] The mother of one of the departing soldiers, overcome with emotion, penned a lengthy poem that was printed in a newspaper two days later. "They are gone! they are gone!" she cried, "to Virginia, the Old Dominion, the home and grave of Washington, to defend it from aggression—our young, our beautiful, our gifted, our gallant corps!—a noble band of valiant brothers of whom Savannah may be justly proud." She signed the poem "A Weeping, Hoping Mother."[38]

Governor Brown had attempted to block the Oglethorpes' departure by issuing orders on May 4 forbidding Georgia troops to take state-issued equipment beyond the state's borders.[39] Bartow brushed aside this obstacle, dashing off a message informing Brown that he was taking his soldiers—and their weapons—to Virginia. Furthermore, Bartow argued, he was demonstrating better than Brown the true spirit of a patriotic Georgian. Bartow declared, "I go to illustrate, if I can, my native State; at all events, to be true to her interests and her character." Bartow's well-chosen words were reprinted in newspapers across the state (and eventually emblazoned on souvenir envelopes offered for sale at the offices of the *Savannah Daily Morning News*[40]), as was Governor Brown's caustic reply on May 29. Brown accused Bartow and his men of shirking their duty and dishonorably abandoning Savannah to less-trained soldiers from other parts of Georgia, while the Oglethorpes sought glory and honor in Virginia. Worst of all, Brown intoned:

You have carried away from Savannah…some of her bravest and best young men, who leave mothers and sisters behind. Should the city be attacked or destroyed in your absence, I fear you could not receive the commendation of those mothers and sisters, whose sons and brothers you took from that city to fill places in Virginia, which thousands of others would gladly have occupied.[41]

Bartow waited more than two weeks, until June 14, before dashing off a blistering answer, penned from camp in Harpers Ferry, Virginia. Clearly, Bartow's anger had heated to the boiling point by the time he wrote to Governor Brown, accusing him of being "criminally ignorant" of the facts and of "stepping out of the way to stab me in the back." Bartow hissed:

I have little time and less inclination to reply in detail to the insolent missive you have thought proper to publish in my absence. Respect, however, for the good opinion of the people of Georgia, induces me, in a few words, to set right my conduct, which you have taken so much pains [sic] to asperse, and to correct the misstatements and false imputations with which your letter abounds.…

You labor, and have constantly labored, under the erroneous impression that YOU are the STATE OF GEORGIA. I beg leave to protest against this conclusion, in which, I assure you, I can never concur.…

I assure you, in passing, that I shall never think it necessary to obtain your consent to enter the service of my country. God forbid that I should ever fall so low.…

I trust, if God spares my life, I shall set foot again on the soil of Georgia, and be well assured that I no more fear to meet my enemies at home than I now do to meet the enemies of my country abroad.[42]

For now, the war of words was over, and preparations for actual combat were underway.

Three days later, Bartow was placed in command of a brigade in General Joseph E. Johnston's Army of the Shenandoah. Bartow's command comprised four regiments of Georgia soldiers as well as smaller numbers of troops from Kentucky and Virginia.[43] General Barnard Bee of South Carolina and a little-known general named Thomas J. Jackson were Johnston's other brigade commanders.[44] Writing to his mother from the vicinity of Winchester, Virginia, on June 23, 1861, Bartow explained, "I am not only in command of a regiment but of a brigade consisting of about 3,000 men. So you see I have a general's command if not the name." The colonel added that his duties permitted him to sleep just five hours per night, and he would "very seldom take off my clothes or even my shoes." Getting dressed in the morning was a matter of simply putting on his hat.[45]

Bartow's soldiers enjoyed camp life and the excitement of military service. One wrote:

> *Our company is the point of attraction....Every evening, and after dress parade, hundreds of the most beautiful ladies can be seen promenading through our camp....We are drilling hard, and should we go to Manassas Gap, I think the O.L.I. will give a good account of themselves....The boys are in good spirits and anxious for a fight.*[46]

Bartow painted a somewhat less cheerful picture in his June 23 letter, admitting, "We have almost marched our shoes off and our breeches out." His soldiers, Bartow said, slept in the open fields for a week and ran so low on food that for two days they could eat only a single meal per day. Still, Bartow bragged, "All are cheerful, all obedient, all ready to sacrifice everything they have if someway [sic] to save the country."

On July 21, one day shy of two months since their much-heralded departure from Savannah, Bartow and his soldiers finally tasted combat in what proved to be the first major battle of the war.[47] The Union and Confederate armies faced off on opposite sides of a creek called Bull Run, a tributary of the Potomac located just over thirty miles west of Washington, D.C. Bartow and one of his regiments, the Eighth Georgia, which included the Oglethorpe Light Infantry, rushed to Matthews Hill to help blunt a fierce Union attack. The fighting was vicious, and six members of the Oglethorpes—all, incredibly, classmates in the same Sunday school class at Savannah's Independent Presbyterian Church—were slain in quick succession. "It was an appalling hour," wrote one participant. "The shot whistled and tore through trees and houses. The ground became literally paved with the fallen....After eight or ten rounds the regiment appeared annihilated."[48] Private Hamilton Branch described the ferocity of the fighting, and one of the deaths, in a letter to his mother four days later:

> *We marched up a hill rite [sic] in the face of the enemy with there [sic] musket balls hailing down all around us. It was here that poor Tom Purse was killed. He was walking in front of me about 10 feet, when he fell on his knees and stuck his head in the ground. I had seen men do the same dodging bomb shells and I thought he was doing the same thing. As I passed*

him, I thought I would look and see who it was and tell him to come on as the balls were raining all around us. I looked and saw he was dead and that it was Tom. [49]

Most dramatic of all was the death of Hamilton Branch's brother Lieutenant John Branch, an officer in the regiment. Startlingly, all three Branch boys—John, Sanford and Hamilton—were on the same battlefield simultaneously; such a situation is practically unthinkable today. Sanford watched in disbelief as John was cut down by an enemy bullet. Sanford described the awful experience in a letter to his mother:

Mother, just think of my horror to see John, Dear John, reel and fall. I dropped my gun and ran to him. I got there just after Dr. West, who Dear John asked whether there was any chance or not. When told he must die, he replied, "Very well—he would die like a soldier and a man."

With the assistance of friends, I carried him to the rear of the regiment....My poor brother lived about ¾ hour. He was perfectly sensible about half the time. He died in my arms. His last words were about you and Hamilton. [50]

Sanford Branch refused to leave his brother's side, even as Union troops overran his position. He was captured, torn away from John's body and taken prisoner. Sanford wrote the agonized lines above from his cell in Washington, D.C.'s Old Capital Prison.

Around 11:30 a.m., Bartow and the remainder of the Eighth Georgia Regiment withdrew from Matthews Hill in disarray along with other Confederate troops, encountering their comrades in the still-intact Seventh Georgia as they retreated. A Union artillery barrage began taking a heavy toll on the remainder of the Southern force, which was now concentrated on Henry Hill, about a mile away from the scene of Colonel Bartow's earlier action. Leaving behind the battered remnants of the Eighth Georgia, Bartow led the Seventh Georgia Regiment into the thick of the fighting on Henry Hill. In so doing, he set in motion a series of events that would claim his life but cement his legend.

The *Savannah Morning News* of July 31, 1932, picks up the narrative:

Bartow...rushed to General Beauregard and asked, "General, what can my brigade do now, and if mortal effort can accomplish it, we will."

The Branch brothers, who followed Colonel Francis Bartow from Savannah to Bull Run. *From left to right*: John, Hamilton and Sanford. *Atlanta History Center.*

"That battery should be silenced," replied Beauregard as he pointed out a spot in the distance from which the enemy's artillery was belching forth death and flame.

Hurrying back to his troops "like a wild man," Bartow was met by Seventh Georgia commander Colonel Lucius Gartrell. Gartrell asked where his men should go, and Bartow replied, "Give me your flag and I will tell you." Bartow raced ahead into a gulley halfway between the Confederate lines and the menacing Union cannons and cried out, "General Beauregard says you must hold this position, and, Georgians, I appeal to you to hold it."[51] Shortly after he uttered these words, a Yankee bullet struck Bartow in the chest just above his heart, mortally wounding him.[52] Bartow fell from his horse, and Georgia soldiers rushed to his side. According to another eyewitness account published in the *Morning News*:

> *They picked him up. With both hands clasped over his breast, he raised his head, and with a God-like effort, his eye glittering in its last gleam with a blazing light, he said, with a last heroic flash of his lofty spirit, "They have killed me, but, boys, NEVER give up the field."—emphasizing the "never" in his peculiar and stirring manner, that all who knew him will so feelingly recall.*[53]

There is considerable disagreement about Bartow's exact words. A newspaper correspondent writing five months later contended that Bartow actually cried, "They have killed me boys; *but never give it up*" (emphasis added). This, said the writer, was a "terser, stronger, and better expression" than the most often quoted version and more characteristic of Bartow's manner of speaking.[54] At least one other correspondent agreed with this version of Bartow's inspiring last words.[55]

The colonel's men carried him back seventy-five to one hundred yards to safety and were forced to move him again due to the ferocity of the enemy fire striking all around. According to the *Savannah Republican*:

> *He drank a little, and then seemed to try to speak, but was not able. They then applied the canteen to his lips a second time, but he was unconscious and could not swallow the water. Laying him back, he died almost instantly, and without a struggle. They took off his gloves and placed them and a cartridge box under his head for a pillow. He did not live more than twenty minutes after he fell.*[56]

According to several period accounts, Bartow breathed his last at 2:00 p.m., though modern historians dispute that claim, asserting that Bartow more likely died no earlier than 3:00 p.m.[57]

Late in the afternoon, Confederate reinforcements arrived by train and broke the Union right flank, turning the tide of the battle and resulting

Grieving mother Charlotte Branch journeyed from Savannah to Virginia to bring her son John's body home from the battlefield. *Atlanta History Center.*

in a disorganized and chaotic Union retreat. The victory provided a big boost for Southern morale, as evidenced in the July 31, 1861 issue of the *Savannah Daily Morning News.* "Victory! Victory! Victory!" the paper trumpeted. "The God of Battles smiles upon the new republican Empire of the South! Eternal justice has been vindicated by our arms, and the fist of God lays bare to the world the wickedness of our oppressors!"[58]

On July 22, with the battlefield safely in Confederate hands, Bartow's troops buried their fallen comrades side by side in a single common grave: Lieutenant Branch, George Butler, Willie Crane, Julius Ferrill, Bryan Morel and Tom Purse. Captain Joseph West, one of the Oglethorpe Light Infantry's officers, presided over a burial service.[59] John Branch's mother, Charlotte, traveled to Virginia to recover her son's body, but she was unable to gain access to John's grave. She remained in Virginia through the fall of 1861, when she returned to Savannah without John's remains.[60]

Bartow's body was scarcely cold before Confederate souvenir hunters descended on the scene, clambering for a memento of his heroic death. According to one correspondent, the battlefield scavengers focused their attention on Bartow's dead horse. "I have been assured," he wrote, "that even the shoes upon his dead horse's feet, (a beautiful gray mare) and several of her teeth, have been removed by persons who wished to obtain some relic of the hero who bestrode her, whilst others have plucked out portions of her mane and tail, and had them wrought into trinkets."[61]

At the completion of the battle, Francis Bartow's remains began a long journey through the Confederacy, leaving Manassas on July 24 for Richmond, where they lay in state in the new Confederate capitol building.[62] The slain officer's face was said to "bear a triumphant expression."[63] From Richmond, the late colonel was carried to Charleston, South Carolina, accompanied by the remains of two other Confederate commanders slain at Manassas, General Bee and Lieutenant Colonel Benjamin Johnson, second in command of Hampton's Legion. According to one eyewitness to the trio's arrival in Charleston, "The cars were appropriately decorated with the Confederate flag and draped in mourning, and the boxes containing the bodies were covered with wreaths made of Laurel, Bay, and Palmetto combined." The train arrived in Charleston on July 26, met by a contingent of local militia troops. Bartow briefly lay in state alongside Bee and Johnson in Charleston's city hall, which was "draped in mourning," as were other public buildings in the city. At 3:00 p.m. on the same day, Bartow's remains were loaded aboard a train bound for Savannah, accompanied by his brother-in-law, Lieutenant John MacPherson Berrien, and a detachment from Company B of the Oglethorpe Light Infantry, a group of young men mustered into service after Bartow and his original soldiers had left Savannah.[64]

The journey by rail to Savannah took five and a half hours, and the spectacle of mourning that greeted Bartow's arrival in Savannah was even greater than the honor accorded to him in Charleston. The funeral train hissed to a stop at 10:30 p.m. on Friday, July 26, at the same station where the late colonel had begun his journey to Virginia with such great fanfare two months earlier. In spite of the late hour, large numbers of citizens lined the streets, standing in silence as Bartow's cortege made its way from the station on West Broad Street to the City Exchange building, which was at the time the seat of Savannah's city government, at the intersection of Bull and Bay Streets. The late-night silence was shattered by the thunder of cannons, firing at one-minute intervals as the coffin moved slowly through the city.[65]

Bartow's coffin was placed inside the council chambers and, according to Mayor Charles C. Jones Jr., "was covered with the Confederate flag and with numerous tokens of respect, such as chaplets of laurel appropriately entwined, the offerings of the ladies of Charleston and of Savannah."[66] An Oglethorpe Light Infantry honor guard stood watch all day on Saturday and into Sunday afternoon, when the body was carried out for Bartow's interment. The solemn pageantry was described in glowing terms the next day in a local newspaper:

The funeral of the lamented Col. Bartow yesterday, was the most solemn and imposing spectacle we ever witnessed in Savannah. At 3 o'clock the military escort was formed on the Bay, composing [sic] all the volunteer companies of the city, with detachments of all the city corps at the forts and fortifications. The remains of Col. Bartow were escorted to Christ Church, which was thronged in every part with citizens, and where the funeral services were conducted by Rt. Rev. Bishop Elliott. At the close of the funeral services, the procession, comprising the military escort, officers of the army and navy, Mayor and Aldermen, family of the deceased, and citizens in carriages, moved up Congress Street to Whitaker, and out Whitaker to Laurel Grove Cemetery, where the remains were, with military honors, consigned to their final resting place....The bells were tolled and minute guns fired, during the march of the procession to the cemetery."[67]

Writing to his parents the next day, Jones concluded, "Colonel Bartow's name will live in the history of these Confederate States, and his noble daring on the field of Manassas be remembered by all."[68]

But Savannah's grieving citizens could not find closure until the remains of the six slain soldiers from Bartow's command were brought home from the battlefield in Virginia, where they had been buried by their comrades.[69] A group of citizens met on the evening of July 23, 1861, and formed a committee of five to go to Manassas and bring back the bodies. They asked the city to help cover the cost of their trip.[70] It would be six months, however, before the goal could be accomplished. It is not clear why it took so long for the bodies to be removed, especially since Charlotte Branch, the mother of Lieutenant John Branch, traveled to Virginia shortly after the battle and was present at a ceremony on the Confederate-held battlefield a month and a half later.[71] The fallen soldiers' eventual arrival in Savannah on February 2, 1862, mirrored Bartow's: the soldiers' bodies arrived on an evening train, and a military honor guard escorted the bodies from the station to the Exchange, where they lay in state in the same room in which Bartow had lain six months earlier. The troops escorted the coffins to Christ Church for another 3:00 p.m. funeral the next day.[72] The young soldiers were perhaps best eulogized by a Virginia newspaper correspondent, who wrote shortly after their deaths the preceding August: "They fought with heroic desperation. All young, all unmarried, all gentlemen, there was not one of the killed who was not an ornament to his community and freighted with brilliant promise."[73]

Bartow's boys—Company A of the Oglethorpe Light Infantry—fought valiantly for the duration of the war, distinguishing themselves in more than thirty battles, including at Gettysburg. Four years of continuous fighting took a terrible toll on the unit. Twenty-eight men were killed, and sixty-five were wounded and discharged. Nine died of noncombat causes, and twenty-eight were promoted out of the ranks. Records indicate that five men—a relatively small number—deserted. At the war's end, just one officer and thirteen soldiers remained, surrendering with General Lee at Appomattox.[74]

For Francis Bartow's widow, the former Louisa Green Berrien, the battlefield death of her husband marked the beginning of a new, more prolonged battle to secure his estate. The late war hero died in debt and without a will, and his wife was saddled with the resulting financial burden. For sixty days, starting on November 8, 1861, the male administrator of Bartow's estate, his former law partner John M.B. Lovell, advertised weekly in the *Savannah Republican* his intent to sell Bartow's property in order to satisfy the creditors. The court appointed appraisers in March 1862, and in October of that year, a judge approved the sale of Bartow's property as follows:

- Ten slaves
- Ten shares of stock in the Savannah Albany Gulf Rail Road Company
- "Certain" (unspecified) real estate in Floyd County, Georgia
- A library of law books

Prior to the sale, in March 1862, Louisa was granted $1,600 cash, the use of a male house slave named Jimmy for one year from the date of Bartow's death, plus furniture and household goods valued at $561.30. Since Bartow was killed in July 1861, Louisa was only able to benefit from the use of her enslaved house servant for about three months. It's uncertain whether Jimmy was sold upon the expiration of the court-ordered term.[75] The disposition of Francis Bartow's large residence at 126 West Harris Street on the northeast corner of Pulaski Square is unclear. The author's perusal of Chatham County real estate deeds revealed no record of the sale of the property, though a more thorough search by a trained deed researcher might yield an answer. The Historic Savannah Foundation purchased the threatened four-story, 8,900-square-foot, twenty-room mansion for less than $18,000 in 1967 and sold it in 1968 to Colonel Lindsey P. Henderson Jr., a military historian who wrote a booklet about Francis Bartow and the Oglethorpe Light Infantry.[76] Henderson claimed that his great-grandfather Thomas Henderson supervised Francis Bartow's funeral, built much of the furniture in Bartow's house and loaned Bartow's widow eighteen wagons and several workers to help her move her belongings out of the house after Bartow's death.[77] Preservationist and antiques dealer Jim Williams, made famous in the 1994 novel *Midnight in the Garden of Good and Evil*, purchased the home from Henderson in 1973 for $32,000.[78] The house was sold in 2014 for just over $2 million and was listed for sale again in early 2016 for $2.5 million.[79]

Francis Bartow's 8,900-square-foot, twenty-room mansion on Savannah's Pulaski Square. *Author's collection.*

Multiple attempts have been made to immortalize Bartow's words and deeds. On September 4, 1861, Bartow's comrades erected what is considered to be the first Confederate battlefield monument of the war. Members of the Eighth Georgia Regiment paid for a white marble shaft, which was laid on the spot where Bartow fell. More than one thousand soldiers marched several miles that morning to reach the location, and shortly after 2:00 p.m.—the time, according to one account, of Bartow's death—a somber ceremony began. A Georgia brass band played a few tunes, a chaplain prayed and the stone was lifted into place. An eyewitness wrote that the shaft was six feet in height, with roughly four feet protruding above the ground after it was erected, and reported that it tapered to a diameter of eight inches at the top.[80] One by one, participants tossed handfuls of dirt at the base of the shaft; officers began the gesture, followed by Charlotte Branch and two other women and then enlisted soldiers. On the shaft were inscribed an uncertain version of Bartow's last words; one eyewitness records that the inscription ended with "Never give up the field!" Another contends the inscription read "Never give up

This 1872 lithograph depicts (somewhat inaccurately) the monument Bartow's troops erected shortly after the battle on the spot where he was mortally wounded. *Library of Congress.*

the fight!" Scholars will likely never know the answer, as the monument all but vanished within months of its appearance.[81]

Southern tourists and souvenir hunters began defacing and even dismantling Bartow's monument shortly after it was erected. A Confederate soldier who took part in the ceremony mailed home a chip from the base of the monument the day after the dedication, instructing the recipient to give the piece to Bartow's sister.[82] Apparently, this memento collector was the first of many. According to a correspondent quoted in the December 24, 1861 issue of the Rome, Georgia *Tri-Weekly Courier*:

I was surprised to find that the marble shaft which marks the spot where the heroic Georgian fell, was covered with the inscriptions of visitors, and that efforts had been made to obtain pieces of it, as mementoes of the man and the field. The inscriptions were written for the most part in pencil, and consisted of the names of the writers, or of some expression of admiration for the gallant dead. One person, more ambitious than the rest, had picked his name into the marble, with the point of a needle or other sharp substance, and had then filled it in with his pencil. The column is literally covered with these inscriptions, not so much space being left as one might cover with his fingernail.[83]

When Southern forces evacuated Manassas in early March 1862, Union troops finished the destructive work begun by Confederate collectors and vandals. On April 29, 1862, a Union soldier wrote of the monument, "At the time I saw it, it was standing & whole, but after a short time, I saw that it had been torn down & the boys were busily at work smashing it in pieces for mementoes [*sic*]."[84] Today, only the weathered stone stump of the former monument remains, wedged between the trunks and roots of two trees that have grown up in the intervening years.

At some point, a small wooden board with a brief inscription was placed on the spot where Bartow died. In 1936, Georgia members of the United Daughters of the Confederacy spearheaded a successful fundraising effort to erect a permanent monument on the site. The stone marker stands several yards away from the original marble shaft and is affixed with a bronze plaque that, curiously, misspells Bartow's middle name: "Stebbings" appears, rather than the correct "Stebbins." The plaque does not recount Bartow's famous last words.

On June 3, 1902, Savannah was the scene of the grandest spectacle honoring Bartow since his death four decades earlier. It was the birthday of Confederate president Jefferson Davis—a state holiday in Georgia in those days. As thousands thronged the streets, a parade comprising hundreds of Confederate veterans and members of the city's various militia units marched north on Drayton Street from the military parade ground in Forsyth Park. A procession of fifteen carriages led the group, which numbered, according to a local newspaper report, close to one thousand. Among the dignitaries riding in the carriages was Bartow's widow, now remarried and living in Atlanta, as well as his sister, a grandniece and a grandnephew. Also included were men who participated in the battle in which Francis Bartow was killed. The throng turned west onto Gaston Street, then north onto Bull Street, stopping at Chippewa Square. Here workers had erected a wooden platform over the fountain that stood in the middle of the square. Flanking the platform to the north and south were two sculptures shrouded in Confederate flags.[85]

When a signal was given, Bartow's grandniece, Miss Frances S. Bartow, pulled away the flag covering the southernmost object, revealing a bronze bust of her forebear perched atop a pedestal of Georgia

Right: Francis Bartow's bust stands today in the shadow of the Confederate Monument in Savannah's Forsyth Park. *Author's collection.*

Below: Chippewa Square circa 1904, six years before bronze busts of Francis S. Bartow and Lafayette McLaws were moved to Forsyth Park. *Library of Congress.*

granite. Sculpted by George Julian Zolnay, known as the "sculptor of the Confederacy" because of his many renderings of Southern leaders, the bust depicted Bartow wearing his Confederate uniform. A second bust on the opposite end of the square, also sculpted by Zolnay, was a likeness of General Lafayette McLaws, who had led Savannah's Confederate veterans' organization after the war.[86] The busts were funded by the veterans, who began raising money in 1899 following McLaws's death. The group also placed nearly identical granite markers over Bartow's and McLaws's graves in Laurel Grove Cemetery. An unsheathed sword and laurel wreath are carved in relief atop each of the sarcophagus-shaped stone markers, and the sides of Bartow's are emblazoned, "I go to illustrate Georgia" and "They have killed me boys, but never give it up." Details of Bartow's death are listed at the foot of the marker.

Bartow and McLaws were forced to give up their places of honor in Chippewa Square in 1910, when Savannahians removed their busts to make way for a statue of Georgia's founder, General James Oglethorpe. They were relocated to the foot of the Confederate Monument in Forsyth Park—perhaps a more appropriate and conspicuous location for a tribute to the two Southern military leaders.

Francis Bartow's ornate, full-length grave marker in Laurel Grove Cemetery, erected by Savannah's Confederate veterans in 1902. *Author's collection.*

Shortly after Bartow's death, a Georgia city and counties in Georgia, Florida and West Virginia were either named or renamed in his honor. Several new military units also branded themselves with the name of the late commander, including Company A, Twenty-Third Regiment, Georgia Volunteer Infantry, colorfully named the "Bartow Yankee Killers."[87] A World War II "Liberty Ship" freighter launched in Savannah in 1944 was christened SS *Francis S. Bartow* eighty-three years and one day after Bartow and his troops boarded their train for Virginia.[88] Also during the war, the U.S. Defense Department named a west Savannah housing complex "Bartow Place." The apartments housed shipyard workers and employees of a military depot in the city. The property was converted to low-income housing after the war. Ironically, considering the slaveholding sympathies of its namesake, it was transformed from "low income white housing" into "Negro housing" in 1960. The complex was demolished in 2005.[89]

The last known tribute to Francis Bartow was an elementary school named for him in east Savannah in 1963. Half a century later, on October 2, 2013, the school was renamed for Otis Brock III, a beloved local school administrator who died of a heart attack at age forty-one the previous year.[90]

Tiny Bartow, Georgia, located more than one hundred miles northwest of Savannah, is named for Francis Bartow, as are counties in Georgia, Florida and West Virginia. *Author's collection.*

Not Yet a Hero

Robert E. Lee's Savannah Sojourns

All rejoice that General Lee has come—we hope in time to save us, under God.
—Reverend Charles C. Jones Sr. to his son, November 14, 1861

Three times, Savannah played an important role in the life of the South's most famous general. It is safe to say the city made as big an impression on the man as he did on it. In fact, Savannah almost cost Robert E. Lee his life.

Lee first arrived in Savannah on November 1, 1829, as a twenty-two-year-old, brand-new U.S. Army engineer lieutenant just graduated from the U.S. Military Academy at West Point. Lieutenant Lee's orders sent him to swampy Cockspur Island, located near the mouth of the Savannah River, twelve miles east of the city. Lee was to help dig a series of embankments, dikes and canals needed to drain the marshy island so a massive new brick fort could be constructed. The work was hard, and the conditions were worse; Lee often stood up to his armpits in sticky mud, harassed by biting insects and tormented by withering heat.[91] Most of the construction was completed by the summer of 1830, when Lee and his workers took a break during Savannah's deadly fever season. When he returned to Cockspur in early November, Lee was horrified to discover that a coastal storm had washed away the embankments, flooded the canal and undone most of his work. Worse, Lee's commanding officer had failed to report for duty; the young, low-ranking engineer was on his own. Lee took charge and completed repairs by the next month.[92] His knowledge of coastal Georgia and its unique geography would come in handy two decades later, when he would command coastal fortifications during the Civil War.

Lee's West Point roommate, Jack Mackay, was a native Savannahian. Thanks to the Mackay family's influence and hospitality, young Lee moved in the city's highest social circles during his 1829–30 Savannah tour of duty. Though Jack was assigned out of state for much of Lee's tenure, Lee socialized regularly with Jack's sisters Margaret, Catherine and Eliza and was often a houseguest at their family's home on Broughton Street between Abercorn and Lincoln Streets. The officer also spent time with Sarah and

Robert E. Lee was a dashing young U.S. Army engineer lieutenant when he was posted at Cockspur Island, outside Savannah, from 1829 to 1831. *Bequest of Robert E. Lee, III, Washington and Lee University, Lexington, Virginia.*

Phillipa Minis, another set of well-heeled Savannah sisters.[93] So pleasant, in fact, were Lee's visits to the city that he gushed about Savannah in a letter to Jack, exclaiming, "That spot of spots! That place of places! That city of cities!"[94] Soon, Lee began courting Eliza Mackay. His most-read biographer, Douglas Southall Freeman, described the relationship between the two: "He was not in love with Eliza Mackay and she had suitors enough…but he was much her cavalier and perhaps he flirted a bit with her."[95] Lee remained on close personal terms with Eliza Mackay even after her marriage to William Henry Stiles in 1854. Lee left Savannah in April 1831, when he was ordered to report to Fortress Monroe, Virginia, to help complete construction work there.[96] A few weeks later, he married his fellow Virginian Mary Custis, with whom he had maintained a long-distance courtship for some time.

When Robert E. Lee returned to Savannah twenty years later in the fall of 1861, he wore not the blue uniform of a U.S. Army engineer but instead the gray coat of a Confederate general. After he turned down supreme command of all Union ground forces at the beginning of the war, Lee's fortunes had suffered when he led a meager Confederate army to defeat at the Battle of Cheat Mountain in southwestern Virginia.[97] Lee was then assigned to command Confederate defenses spread over three hundred miles of Atlantic coastline in South Carolina, Georgia and Florida, including his former post on Cockspur Island, where twenty-five million bricks had been stacked atop the dike system Lee helped construct.[98] The seemingly impregnable fortification that resulted, Fort Pulaski, was named for a Polish hero of the 1779 Revolutionary War Battle of Savannah. But not even the stout brick walls of this massive fort could cheer General Lee, whose mood was as gray as his uniform. Writing to his youngest daughter, Mildred, Lee darkly described his new assignment as "another forlorn hope expedition. Worse than West Virginia."[99]

At first, events seemed to bear out Lee's dour prophecy. On November 7, 1861, as General Lee was making his way to his new base of operations, more than twelve thousand Union troops, backed by a fleet of seventy-seven U.S. Navy warships, drove out the three thousand Confederate soldiers garrisoning two earthen fortifications in Hilton Head, South Carolina. It was a terrible blow for the Confederates; in addition to the loss of their arms and supplies, the Southerners now had to contend with a new Union foothold lodged halfway between Charleston and Savannah. Port Royal became the headquarters of the U.S. Navy's South Atlantic Blockading Fleet and was used as the springboard for countless incursions into Confederate territory throughout the war. Lee clearly foresaw the danger, writing to South Carolina governor Andrew McGrath: "Our enemy increases in strength faster than we do & is now enormous. Where he will strike I do not know, but the blow when it does fall will be hard."[100]

Lee's task was made nearly insurmountable by the nature of the geography within his command. The coastal barrier islands were separated from the mainland by miles of salt marshes and meandering streams, providing innumerable avenues by which the powerful enemy fleet could attack. To defend against this required either a strong navy—which the Confederacy did not have—or fortifications virtually everywhere. The latter option was impossible for any military, let alone a new force hastily created with limited resources. Lee quickly realized he would need to pick and choose which points to defend, and he knew his decisions would likely prove unpopular with an unsympathetic public that failed to grasp its predicament.[101] He explained to Confederate secretary of war Judah P. Benjamin: "I exceedingly dislike to yield an inch of territory to our enemies. They are, however, able to bring such large & powerful batteries to whatever point they please, that it becomes necessary for us to concentrate our strength."[102] Clinging to exposed positions would only invite a repeat of the blistering and costly defeat at Hilton Head.

Lee ordered the abandonment of the barrier islands and the burning or destruction of any resources that could not be moved. Confederate soldiers put the Tybee Island and St. Simons Island lighthouses to the torch and even set much of the evacuated city of Brunswick, Georgia, ablaze.[103] Engineers transferred cannons from the exposed batteries into a newly constructed inner line of earthen fortifications closer to the cities, ports and railroads. Simultaneously, they put in place a series of impassable obstructions, such as wooden pilings and massive, stone-filled boxes, called "cribs," to slow down or block any attempted Union naval movement up the rivers. Lee's overall strategy was to make it costly and difficult for the U.S. Navy to attempt another big attack like the one that captured Port Royal.[104] The plan worked, for Savannah held firm, remaining in Confederate hands until Union general William T. Sherman's "March to the Sea" brought overwhelming numbers of troops from the opposite direction. Savannah owes its four years of Southern control largely to the strong interior line of defensive fortifications and river obstructions created by General Lee.[105]

During his time in command on the coast, Lee labored against a grumbling, stubborn populace that, incredibly, seemed unaware of the danger they faced. The general complained about this frequently in letters to his children. On December 8, 1861, he wrote, "The people do not seem to realize there is a war." He added on March 1 of the following year:

Our people have not been earnest enough, have thought too much of themselves & their ease, & instead of turning out to a man, have been content to nurse themselves & their dimes, & leave the protection of themselves & families to others. To satisfy their conscience, they have been clamorous in criticizing what others have done, & endeavoured to prove that they ought to do nothing. This is not the way to accomplish our independence.[106]

Lee returned to Cockspur Island to visit Fort Pulaski on at least three occasions during this period. The first time was on November 10, 1861.[107] The newly arrived general made an impression on twenty-four-year-old Colonel Charles H. Olmstead, the fort's commander. "He would have been recognized any where [*sic*] in the world as a man of mark, one upon whom Nature had set the stamp of greatness," Olmstead remembered. Extoling Lee's physical frame and facial features in cloyingly hagiographical terms, Olmstead concluded, "He met my highest conception of ideal manhood....A

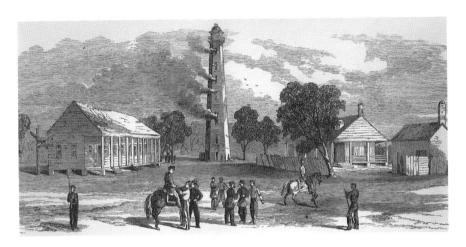

Confederate soldiers put the Tybee Island Lighthouse to the torch in early 1862 when General Lee ordered coastal fortifications abandoned or destroyed. *Coastal Heritage Society, Savannah.*

great and good man if God ever made one."[108] While it is worth noting that Olmstead penned his description of Lee years later, after the general had been elevated to the status of near-sainthood in the former Confederate States, it is nonetheless clear that Lee's arrival in Savannah did much to reassure this young officer who was about to face trial by fire.

Lee's aim in visiting Fort Pulaski was to assess the strength of this bastion of Savannah's Confederate defenses and suggest ways to make it stronger, for it was all but certain that Union forces would follow up their victory at Port Royal with ever-deeper incursions into coastal Georgia and South Carolina. Lee surveyed Olmstead's preparations and offered several suggestions to protect the troops inside the fort, including erecting timber walls throughout the interior to guard against flying shell fragments and digging ditches and pits in the large central open area to catch enemy projectiles. Before departing, General Lee gave young Colonel Olmstead some reassuring words, which Olmstead recounted in his memoirs: "'They' (the enemy) will make it pretty hot for you with shells, but they cannot breach your walls at that distance.' I have remembered his words particularly because of subsequent events which proved how mistaken they were."[109] Lee was not alone in his failure to foresee the range and accuracy of the new rifled artillery shells, which made the unthinkable possible. Firing from concealed positions just under one mile away on Tybee Island, Union artillerymen were able to compel Fort Pulaski to surrender on

April 11, 1862. Though the city, as noted, remained under Confederate command, the fall of Fort Pulaski gave Union forces complete control of the main entrance to Savannah from the sea, tightening the blockade and keeping the city effectively bottled up for the remainder of the war.

General Lee's assignment to Savannah nearly cost him his life. Sometime in early 1862, Lee traveled to Fort Bartow, an earthen fortification at Causton's Bluff, east of the city. This sprawling artillery installation, which spread over seventeen acres at the point of land where St. Augustine Creek and the Wilmington River converge near the Savannah River, mounted sixteen cannons.[110] The purpose of Lee's visit was to observe the test-firing of a massive new gun that Confederate designers hoped would be able to accurately throw a projectile at targets up to five miles away. With sudden, deadly violence, the new cannon exploded, hurling a huge chunk of its iron barrel toward the group of observers. The flying piece of shrapnel barely missed Lee's head, but it killed or injured several other men who were standing nearby. The massive cannon fragment splashed down in the marsh mud more than one thousand feet away.[111]

Sometime in the late twentieth century, the fragment—or at least a huge chunk of metal closely matching its description, and clearly a piece of some large cannon—began to protrude from the mud of the Wilmington River. Local boaters took notice, and authorities feared the artifact might eventually be damaged or destroyed. At low tide on January 11, 2000, experts from the Coastal Heritage Society used a fourteen-ton crane to hoist the three-thousand-pound cannon fragment out of the mud. They hauled the heavy remnant to nearby Old Fort Jackson, a National Historic Landmark site operated by the society. Conservators scraped off oyster shells that had accumulated over more than a century in the brackish river, submerged the big artifact in fresh water and subjected it to several years of electric current to stabilize the iron enough to expose it once again to oxygen. Today, visitors to Fort Jackson may stand inches away from the remains of the cannon that almost decapitated the Confederacy's most famous general and wonder how differently things might have turned out—for both sides—if Lee had been standing just a few inches closer to the big weapon that day in 1862.[112]

In spite of his heavy workload and regular travel between far-flung points on the coast, Lee was able to rekindle many friendships from his days as a young lieutenant in Savannah two decades earlier. His youthful flirtation with Eliza Mackay (now Stiles) had blossomed into a mature friendship. In fact, Eliza even offered to help Lee mend his worn clothing. The general wrote to his daughter Annie in March 1862: "Mrs. S has undertaken to

This large iron fragment, on exhibit at Old Fort Jackson outside Savannah, is believed to be part of the cannon that exploded during a test firing at Fort Bartow in early 1862, nearly striking General Lee. *Author's Collection.*

repair my shirts & necessity has compelled me to accept her offer, which I am ashamed to do, both on account of the trouble to her & the exhibition of my rags. But pride must have a fall."[113]

And so, too, must every military posting come to an end. Under orders from Confederate president Jefferson Davis, Lee departed Savannah for Richmond, Virginia, on March 3, 1862, and assumed command of the struggling Army of Northern Virginia three months later. Under Lee's capable leadership, the force became legendary.[114] Eight long years passed before Lee returned to Savannah, as part of a two-month journey through several Southern states in the spring of 1870. Lee's health had declined greatly since the end of the war, and he took a break from his duties as president of Virginia's Washington College in hopes that travel would restore his constitution. Alas, neither Eliza nor her brother Jack, Lee's West Point roommate, were waiting to greet the former general when he arrived in the city that was the scene of so many of their shared fond memories. Jack Mackay died in 1848, two years after illness forced him to resign from the army, and Eliza passed away in 1867.[115]

Hundreds of Savannahians were waiting when Lee's train hissed to a stop at the Central of Georgia Railway Station on West Broad Street—the same station that saw Francis S. Bartow's triumphant departure for Virginia in 1861 and his return in a coffin several weeks later. After acknowledging the

During his April 1870 visit to Savannah, General Lee posed for this portrait with fellow former Confederate general Joseph E. Johnston, who was living in Savannah at the time. *Library of Congress.*

cheers of the throng of admirers, which even included soldiers from the U.S. Army force occupying the conquered city, Lee and his thirty-year-old daughter Agnes climbed aboard an open-topped carriage and rode to the home of former Confederate general Alexander Lawton on the southwest trust lot on Oglethorpe Square. Lee enjoyed a dinner with Lawton and other ex-Confederate commanders. When the meal was finished, an exhausted Lee left for the home of Savannah merchant Andrew Low, Eliza Mackay's son-in-law, on Lafayette Square.

Shortly after Lee's surreptitious departure, two local marching bands appeared on Lawton's doorstep, accompanied by a mob of about one thousand Confederate veterans. The bands alternated their performances, taking turns with renditions of patriotic songs such as "Dixie," "Bonnie Blue Flag" and even "Hail to the Chief." General Lawton graciously acknowledged the men's compliment, averring that the aging General Lee much appreciated the serenade but had retired for the evening and could not express his thanks in person. Lawton tactfully omitted the fact that Lee had left the house and was now staying elsewhere. The marching celebrants proceeded to the East Oglethorpe Street home of former Confederate general Joseph E. Johnston, who had moved to Savannah two years earlier to operate an insurance agency. Subsequent stops included performances at the homes of General Henry Rootes Jackson and finally Colonel John Screven, Savannah's mayor.[116]

General Lee spent three weeks in Savannah, not including a brief side trip to Florida.[117] He visited many old friends and even sat with General Johnston for a portrait by local photographer David J. Ryan, probably inside the photographer's studio at the corner of Congress and Whitaker Streets.[118] The aging generals both dressed in dark suits with wide lapels. Lee appears to have sported a long necktie, more modern than Johnston's bow tie. Lee's shoes were polished to a shine. Johnston's, casually crossed, were dull and sensible. Both of the aging generals wore beards. Lee's hair, snow-white, was cropped short on the sides, rather than curling into the characteristic wisps over his ears. The two men sat on opposite sides of a small table—Johnston in a wooden armchair, Lee in a pedestaled office chair. The commanders stared blankly into each other's eyes, Lee's right hand gripping a dip pen apparently frozen in midsentence, Johnston's holding open the pages of a book. Copies of this and two similar photographs were printed and sold to raise money for the Ladies Memorial Association, which was planning a Confederate monument in Savannah.[119] While it is occasionally claimed that the Savannah portrait was the last photo taken of Lee, the general actually posed once more, in Richmond in June 1870, for pictures to be used by the sculptor creating his bust.[120]

When Robert E. Lee climbed aboard a Charleston-bound train on Monday morning, April 25, he bade his final farewell to the city where he began his active duty military career four decades earlier and honed his skills as a planner and commander in the first full year of the Civil War.[121] The great general suffered a stroke in Virginia late the following September and died on October 12, 1870.

4

CSS *ATLANTA*

Savannah's "Iron Monster"

What a comfortless, infernal, and God-forsaken ship!!
—*diary of Midshipman Dabney Minor Scales, Confederate States Navy, April*
14, 1863

On November 12, 1861, a much-anticipated vessel slid triumphantly up the Savannah River. The *Fingal*, a Scottish-built merchant ship noteworthy for its unusual iron hull, carried Confederate secret agent James D. Bulloch, whose exploits in Europe would eventually make him legendary. Packed into the hold were fifteen thousand rifles, three thousand swords, five hundred pistols, four advanced rifled cannons, thousands of pounds of gunpowder and millions of rounds of ammunition—all of it snuck past the Union warships manning the blockade off the Georgia coast. The *Fingal's* cargo was a windfall for the resource-starved Confederate military.[122] As the *Fingal* came within sight of the waterfront warehouses of Savannah between 2:30 and 3:00 p.m., the crew fired two cannon shots to announce their arrival and dropped anchor abreast of the Exchange building near the foot of Whitaker Street. It seemed as if "the whole population of the town was out" to greet the ship, remembered one passenger.[123]

The arrival of the *Fingal* and its cargo was a much-needed shot in the arm for Savannahians, whose morale was sagging following the fall of two Confederate fortifications in nearby Port Royal, South Carolina, to Union forces five days earlier. Savannahian Edward C. Anderson, who sailed to Georgia aboard the *Fingal* after completing his mission as a Confederate secret agent in Europe, noted in his journal: "I found the people of Savannah frightened to death by the capture of Port Royal; indeed there was good reason for them to be so, for there was really nothing to prevent the Yankees from following up their success and coming straight to the city. The arrival of the *Fingal* restored confidence to everybody."[124]

Unfortunately for the Confederate cause, the Union navy heavily built up Port Royal, creating a strong, deep-water base for blockading operations halfway between the key Southern ports of Savannah and Charleston. When the *Fingal*, loaded with Southern cotton intended for sale in friendly European ports, attempted to get back to sea two days before Christmas, Union gunboats blocked its way and forced the blockade runner to return to Savannah.[125] No additional opportunities presented themselves in the ensuing months, and all hope of escape was finally snuffed out when massive Fort Pulaski, fifteen miles from Savannah at the mouth of the Savannah River, fell to Union rifled artillery attack on April 11, 1862. While it was still possible for blockade runners like the *Fingal* to escape, the combination of multiple Union gunboats and dangerously shallow water made the prospect highly unlikely. "I will cork up Savannah like a bottle," boasted Rear Admiral Samuel F. Du Pont, the top U.S. Navy commander in the region, in late November. Eleven days later, Du Pont announced, "Savannah is completely stopped up."[126] The Union strategy proved so successful that later in the war, even a Confederate commander noted wistfully, "There is no part of the Atlantic coast which may be more effectually blockaded than Savannah."[127]

With the *Fingal* essentially trapped—to expand on Du Pont's metaphor—like a ship in a bottle, Confederate authorities shifted their focus from blockade-running to warship-building. They began making plans to convert the iron-hulled merchantman into a powerful ironclad fighting ship along the lines of the CSS *Virginia*, which had menaced the Union blockading fleet in Hampton Roads, Virginia, in March 1862. In that instance, Confederate shipbuilders salvaged the hull of the burned, scuttled U.S. Navy ship *Merrimack*, whose engines and machinery survived, and topped the wooden hull with a slope-sided, fortress-like iron box called a casemate. Renamed CSS *Virginia*, the new ironclad warship steamed into action on March 9, 1862, destroying two enemy vessels before it was checkmated by the arrival of the Union ironclad USS *Monitor* the next day. The *Virginia* and *Monitor* became prototypes for dozens of additional warships built by both navies throughout the war; most subsequent Confederate ironclads featured iron casemates like the *Virginia*'s, and the bulk of the Union vessels were characterized by flat-decked, armored hulls topped with rotating iron gun turrets like the *Monitor*'s.

The Confederate navy engaged entrepreneurial brothers Nelson and Asa Tift to oversee the conversion and refit of the *Fingal*. These Connecticut-born, Southern-bred siblings had all but finished the mega-ironclad CSS *Mississippi* in New Orleans, only to be forced to intentionally torch the incomplete vessel to keep it out of enemy hands when the port city fell to Union forces in April 1862. The Tifts needed a new project for their considerable talents, and Confederate Secretary of the Navy Stephen Mallory offered them the *Fingal*. The brothers agreed to donate their time and effort, asking only that they be allowed to construct the ship as they saw fit, without any interference from local naval commanders—the same arrangement under which they had labored in New Orleans. Mallory agreed, and on May 7, 1862, the steamship *General Lee* towed the now-emptied *Fingal* twenty miles upriver to the little village of Purysburg, South Carolina (sometimes spelled "Purrysburg").[128]

The Tifts' workers spent two months stripping the *Fingal*. They removed all the passenger and crew cabins and other structures down to the main deck, leaving the ship's iron hull and top-of-the-line steam engines and machinery in place. Then they began converting the former merchant vessel into the Confederacy's most menacing warship. In order to accommodate the iron-armored casemate, the builders expanded the *Fingal*'s width by 6 feet on each side via wooden extensions called sponsons. The resulting ironclad, christened CSS *Atlanta*, was 204 feet long and 41 feet wide. Its hull rose up about 2 feet out of the water and was covered up by iron armor that hung down over the sides of the ship several feet into the water. The casemate sides were 8 feet tall, slanted back twenty-nine degrees, resulting in an armored enclosure that stood 6 feet from top to bottom. The walls of this floating fortress were stoutly built from eighteen inches of crisscrossed southern oak and pine, on the outside of which were fastened two layers of iron armor totaling four inches in thickness. The ship itself was a weapon, with a bow terminating in a stout iron beak that could be used to ram enemy warships—a particularly lethal tactic against soft wooden hulls. The *Atlanta*'s helmsman would steer the ship from inside an iron-armored pilothouse that rose 3 feet above the casemate's top—called the spar deck—which was also armored.[129]

The *Atlanta*'s casemate was pierced by eight gun ports—three on each side and one on each end. One rifled cannon was permanently mounted on each

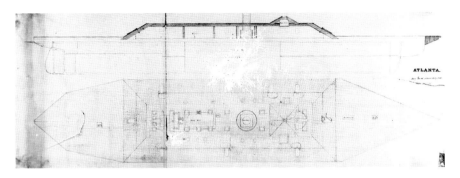

Plans of the CSS *Atlanta*, apparently drawn up after the captured Confederate ironclad was being refitted at the U.S. Navy Yard in Philadelphia. *Naval History and Heritage Command.*

side, while the other two cannons could be rotated to fire out of gun ports on the bow and stern (front and back) or from the sides of the ship. The cannons—called "rifled guns" in the military terminology of the day—were of an advanced type that utilized grooves cut into the insides of the barrels to fire projectiles accurately at great distances. The gun ports were protected by heavy iron shutters that pivoted open from their upper corners to allow the cannons to be rolled out and fired, then pulled back inside and reloaded in relative safety with the port shutter closed. The pièce de résistance was a frightening invention known as a "spar torpedo"—a powerful explosive device attached to the end of a long wooden pole extending underwater from the front of the ship, which the crew could raise and lower by means of a lever operated inside the *Atlanta*.[130]

Not surprisingly, even with its heavy masts and sails removed, the additional weight of all the new iron armor changed the way the ship handled. The first consequence was a loss of speed, from a maximum of roughly twelve miles per hour as the *Fingal* to, on average, slightly more than half that fast as the *Atlanta*. The new warship was also difficult to steer, with its bulky six-foot-wide sponsons causing it to handle clumsily, like a big wooden raft—a dangerous characteristic for a warship needing to maneuver quickly and accurately in close combat. But the biggest drawback to the *Atlanta*'s configuration was its increased draft, which caused the ship to ride fifteen feet below the surface of the water. Since most of the passages that would allow the *Atlanta* to access open ocean from Savannah were no more than fourteen feet deep on a normal high tide, the ship would be required to wait for the twice-monthly extra-high tides known as "spring tides" to go to sea. When coal, required to operate the *Atlanta*'s steam engines, was loaded for the first time, the added weight pushed the ship two feet deeper into the river, and water seeped in so rapidly that the living spaces below decks were flooded to a depth of one foot. One of the ship's officers wrote that after the influx, "There was hardly a dry bed in the ship."[131] The end result of this handicap was that *Atlanta* would have to begin a voyage riding high in the water, with up to two feet of normally submerged unarmored hull exposed, and have coal loaded later, when it was in deeper water. Largely because of the leaks, close to four months passed between the *Atlanta*'s first shakedown cruise toward Fort Pulaski on July 31, 1862, and the ship's official commissioning on November 22.[132]

Unlike its earlier incarnation, the luxurious civilian steamship *Fingal*, the ironclad warship *Atlanta* was a miserable place to live and work. One observer noted "the roughness of all the work" aboard the ship, suggesting, "The comfort of the crew and its sanitary condition appear to have been totally disregarded. Efficiency in battle seems to have been the sole point aimed at." The spaces below decks were poorly ventilated, he continued, "rendering them almost uninhabitable in hot weather." The *Atlanta*'s own officers were even more pointed in their criticism of the ship's lack of creature comforts. "The officers quarters are the most uncomfortable that I have ever seen," Midshipman Dabney Scales griped in his diary. He continued: "They are so dark as to require lights to be kept burning continually, and there are no staterooms in either cabins, wardroom, or steerage. The apartments are partitioned off with coarse, half-worn, dirty canvas." Master Thomas Littlepage echoed Scales's complaints, declaring: "I would defy anyone in the world to tell when it is day or when night if he is confined below without any way of marking time....I would venture to say that if a person were blindfolded and carried below and then turned loose he would imagine himself in a swamp, for the water is trickling in all the time and everything is so damp." "What a *comfortless, infernal, and God-*

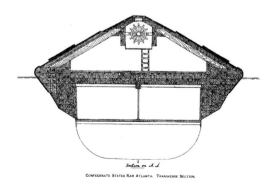

A cross section showing the sponsons, which extended out over the sides of the hull to accommodate the ship's iron armor. *Official Records of the Union and Confederate Navies in the War of the Rebellion.*

forsaken ship!!" wailed Scales on April 14, 1863, emphasizing the words in his diary.[133]

The unfortunate Confederate navy officers were not the only people sleeping poorly thanks to the appearance of the CSS *Atlanta*. Union authorities had closely monitored the *Fingal's* conversion into an ironclad and were gravely concerned about the threat the new *Atlanta* posed to their blockading fleet, based twenty-five miles up the coast in Port Royal. "She is the finest and most powerful vessel the Confederates have ever had," noted *Harper's Weekly*, and a correspondent for the *New York Herald* warned that unless a U.S. Navy *Monitor* class ironclad were dispatched to Port Royal soon, the wooden warships anchored in the bay would have "an excellent opportunity of learning what it is to be blown out of the water."[134]

Little did these Northern commentators know of the difficulties the *Atlanta's* Confederate commanders were facing in their efforts to pay a visit to Port Royal. The Southerners made multiple attempts to take their brand-new warship to sea, but they were stymied every time—either by Mother Nature, human interference or simple bad luck. The *Atlanta* made its first attempted combat sortie down the Savannah River on January 5, 1863. The ship's surgeon, Dr. Robert Gibbes, eagerly anticipated "a furious raid with our Iron Monster on the God-forsaken foe."[135] Much to Gibbes's surprise, it was the *Atlanta* that was forsaken. The ship could not get over or around the man-made obstructions—massive stone-filled wooden boxes called "cribs"—that Confederate military engineers had placed in the river to thwart Union attacks. The day had gotten off to a promising start, with a heavy fog offering the ironclad a cloak of invisibility to mask its attack, but it ended in bitter disappointment for the captain and crew. Midshipman Scales wrote in his diary, "We all on board had the mortification to see the anchor again dropped in Savannah River, with the certainty of remaining here till the next spring tide, and probably much longer."[136]

When the army's removal efforts failed, the Confederate navy gave shipbuilder Nelson Tift a shot at uprooting the stubborn obstacles. Tift first tried lashing one of the rock-filled stone cribs to barges in an attempt to use the rising tide to float the obstruction out of the way. When that didn't work, he resorted to explosive methods, employing hundreds of pounds of gunpowder. Tift set off bigger and bigger blasts until he'd cleared a path for the *Atlanta* to pass. Unfortunately, another high tide had come and gone, and the hapless ship and its crew would have to wait a bit longer.[137]

New plans were laid for the *Atlanta* to break out of Savannah at the next high tide on February 4, but a few days before the beginning of the mission, a second Union ironclad warship, the monitor *Passaic*, arrived in Wassaw Sound, right in the *Atlanta*'s intended path. It was possible the Confederate ironclad could have steamed past the single Union monitor already on station, but fighting its way past two of the enemy ships was considered more than the *Atlanta* could handle. Even if Commodore Josiah Tattnall, the top Confederate naval commander in Savannah at the time, had been willing to make the attempt, it is possible the tides would have prevented the *Atlanta* from sailing past the obstructions. Midshipman Scales reported in his diary that winds from a strong storm the night before had prevented the water level from rising high enough to allow the ironclad to pass. "So," he lamented, "we [are] once again disappointed." Commodore Tattnall was able to usefully employ the *Atlanta* and its powerful battery to provide protection while the Confederate army repositioned land-based cannons at Causton's Bluff outside the city, but it was hardly enough to placate angry Savannahians impatient for action. Scales fretted about how the new delays might damage the reputation of the *Atlanta* and its crew. "Of course we will be branded as cowards by the unthinking portion of the citizens of Savannah for not going down and destroying the enemy's ironclad," fumed Scales. "These people never stop to enquire into the cause [of] these delays, but stigmatize the navy generally, because we did not go down and sink the enemy's fleet, even before the obstructions had been removed from the river."[138]

Tenacious Commodore Tattnall refused to give up. After several days, he moved the *Atlanta* back to Wassaw Sound to prepare for another attempt to break out of Savannah. Tattnall's plans were revealed to the enemy when, on March 19, a handful of foreign-born sailors aboard a small Confederate navy picket boat grabbed their officer's weapon and announced their intention to switch sides. The men rowed their vessel to Union-held Fort Pulaski, where they revealed information about the upcoming cruise of the CSS *Atlanta*. U.S. Army colonel Charles Halpine passed the information along to U.S. Navy authorities in Port Royal, and Admiral Samuel F. Du Pont responded by rushing two additional *Monitor* class ironclads, the *Weehawken* and *Nahant*, down to Savannah to block the Confederate vessel's path.[139] Eventually, Du Pont recalled the two new monitors in preparation for a massive naval attack on Confederate forces in Charleston Harbor, but the absence of the Union ironclads did little to change the *Atlanta*'s fortunes. The Confederate ship ran aground again on March 30 and was stuck for twelve hours. It took the combined efforts of three steam-powered wooden vessels to pull the *Atlanta* free, and afterward, the warship's crew was compelled to run the two bilge pumps around the clock for two weeks to drain out all the water that had seeped into the ship.[140]

After so many thwarted attempts to employ their new warship, Confederate authorities and Savannah's populace were nearly apoplectic with frustration. A clamor arose to sack Tattnall and other older officers and replace them with younger, more active commanders who would get the *Atlanta* into action. Savannah banker and businessman Gazaway Bugg Lamar fumed in a letter to Confederate navy secretary Stephen Mallory, "What is the use of building Iron Clads at enormous expense, that then remain idle—better not to build them, & have no officers— you would save much money—& our cause prosper just as well without either." In a subsequent letter, Lamar groused that the *Atlanta* "was completed early in December last & has done nothing—not one red copper's worth, since— & in my opinion, she never will, under the control of Old Fogeyism here."[141] Partly in response to the outcry from citizens like Lamar, thirty-eight-year-old Commander William Webb was promoted and brought in to take charge of the Savannah Squadron. According to Edward C. Anderson, who had served with Webb in the prewar U.S. Navy, Webb "was boastful and disinclined to listen to the counsel of older, wiser heads than his own."[142]

William A. Webb, commander of the CSS *Atlanta*, was considered by his peers to be bold but reckless. *Courtesy of Dr. Maurice Melton.*

Commander Webb had more experience than most Confederate officers in fighting Union monitors and had good reason to believe these iron monsters were less fearsome than many people believed. As captain of the little wooden gunboat *Teaser*, Webb had been involved up close in the first great ironclad battle between the CSS *Virginia* and USS *Monitor* in Hampton Roads the previous year. He had watched the *Virginia* challenge the *Monitor* repeatedly in subsequent encounters and observed that the *Monitor*'s commander never chose to engage. Webb had witnessed land-based Confederate artillery pummeling two Union ironclads at Drewry's Bluff, Virginia, driving them away, in May 1862. He was aware that the

Monitor-class ironclad USS *Montauk* had been unable to defeat earthen Fort McAllister south of Savannah, and Webb had personally witnessed the blistering defeat dealt to the massed Union ironclad fleet by the Confederate defenders in Charleston Harbor on April 7, 1863.[143] It is little wonder Webb believed that, as commander of the Confederacy's most powerful warship, he could hold his own against more than one monitor.

Webb got underway on May 30 and almost immediately suffered the same fate as every other man who had attempted to take the CSS *Atlanta* to sea—he ran aground, this time because of an engine breakdown. It took a full twenty-four hours to pull the ship free of the mud. Then, in a scenario sickeningly similar to the events of the previous March, deserting Confederate soldiers once again fled to Union-held Fort Pulaski, alerting their interrogators to the *Atlanta*'s movements. This time, Admiral Du Pont sent two monitors, USS *Weehawken* and USS *Nahant*, to Wassaw Sound, blocking Webb's path to the sea.[144] At this point, even the normally hawkish navy secretary Mallory became slightly cautious, suggesting that perhaps Webb should wait to strike until he could be joined by the new ironclad CSS *Savannah*, which had just been completed and was awaiting the installation of its cannons. Wouldn't two ironclads be stronger than one—and safer, too? Webb's reply was typically bullish. "In my opinion it is so uncertain when she [the *Savannah*] will be ready for active service that I have determined not to depend on her to act with me," he announced. "I propose then, with your approval, to leave in the *Atlanta*, whether the *Savannah* is ready or not, on the next full moon tides." Assuring Mallory that "the whole abolition fleet has no terror for me," Webb outlined an outlandish plan to use the *Atlanta* "to break up and raise the blockade between here and Charleston," stop by Port Royal, "damaging the enemy there as much as possible," then steam straight up the Savannah River and place Fort Pulaski under siege.[145]

Over the next week, Webb had the good sense to lower his expectations—but just a little bit. He decided he would fight the two monitors on his own but wait until the *Savannah* could join forces with the *Atlanta* to tackle the remainder of the Union fleet.[146] With very little coal in his bunkers, Webb got underway at 6:00 p.m. on Wednesday, June 17, 1863. Two hours later, after successfully clearing the Confederate obstructions, he dropped anchor in the Wilmington River and began taking on a full load of coal. The dirty, laborious process of loading the fuel onto the ship took all night; and, as expected, the weight of the coal pushed the *Atlanta* deeper into the treacherously shallow water. About dark, Webb moved the ship downriver, stopping for the night about five or six miles from where he expected the enemy to be waiting. The stage was set for the Confederacy's most powerful new warship finally to make her entrance into battle.[147]

At 3:30 on the morning of June 17, Webb made his move. His plan was to strike the first monitor he encountered with the *Atlanta*'s spar torpedo, blasting a hole in the Union ship's vulnerable hull. Then he would turn his attention to the other Yankee ironclad and batter it into submission with his rifled cannons, which were accurate at greater distances than the monitors' bigger but less-advanced smoothbore guns. Two wooden steam-powered Confederate warships, the *Isondiga* and *Resolute*, followed some distance in *Atlanta*'s wake; their job was to engage any wooden blockading vessels, such as the gunboat USS *Cimarron*, that the *Atlanta* might encounter, and then to tow the captured monitors back up the river to Savannah.[148] Aboard the *Atlanta*, Commander Webb roused his men with a stirring pep talk, informing them it was their duty to capture both of the enemy ironclads. According to crewman John W. Carey, Webb's closing words were "Boys, all I ask of you is don't say stop too soon."[149]

The two Union monitors were anchored in the mouth of Wassaw Sound (frequently spelled "Warsaw Sound" in period documents), ready to strike when the Confederate ironclad appeared. Aboard the USS *Weehawken*, Captain John Rodgers spotted the *Atlanta* and its consorts headed his way at 4:10 a.m. He had been expecting the Confederate ironclad and attached a float to his anchor so he could cut it loose quickly and get underway immediately, without taking time to raise the anchor and bring it on board.[150] Aboard the *Nahant*, seventeen-year-old crewman Alvah Folsom Hunter saw the quartermaster come "running-tumbling down the ladder. He seized the boatswain's mate by the arm and exclaimed: 'Call all hands, quick, sound to quarters. She's coming right down upon us!'" Clambering up onto the monitor's deck, Hunter beheld the onrushing attacker with his own eyes:

About a mile distant was the Ram coming down towards us at a fast clip, as was evident from "the bone in her teeth" (the jet of foam turned up by her bow), and I could distinctly see a small spar standing almost straight up from a light framework on her bow, with a black object about the size of a nail-keg on top of it. This last I "sensed" at once was a spar-torpedo....I saw the spar on the bow of the Ram swing forward and down and drop into the water with a splash.[151]

Since the tide was outbound, the current had pushed both monitors around so their bows faced the sea. By 4:30, both Union ironclads were underway single file, headed straight for the *Atlanta*. The *Nahant* followed behind *Weehawken*, since only the latter carried a pilot with knowledge of the area's dangerous waterways.[152]

At this point, the *Atlanta*'s old, familiar enemy—its own deep draft—struck. According to *Atlanta* crewman Thomas Veitch, Webb had asked his pilots if there was enough water beneath the ship for him to ram or torpedo one of the monitors; when answered in the affirmative, the commander ordered the attack. Veitch may have been implying that Webb elected to steer the *Atlanta* out of the deep water of the channel. If so, his calculated risk failed.[153] When the ironclad was within three-quarters of a mile of the enemy ships, its hull hit the bottom and stuck fast. Fortunately, the tide was still rising, and the ship floated free fifteen minutes later—but Webb and his crew were crestfallen when the *Atlanta* grounded in the mud and sand again. The heartbreaking cycle repeated itself at least once more, but the ship was never able to break free and move under its own power again for the duration of the ensuing battle.[154] In his official account of the action, Webb recounted, "All this time we were hard and fast aground."[155]

It was 4:55 a.m. Seeing the *Weehawken*, still a mile and a half away, steaming toward his stranded, immobile ship, Webb ordered the commander of his forward pivot gun to fire. A lucky shot, he hoped, might stop the monitor in its tracks and force it to fight from a distance. Farther away, Alvah Hunter watched the action from the deck of the *Nahant*:

> The black muzzle of a gun appeared out of the bow porthole; in two or three seconds there was a flash from the gun and a shot struck the water perhaps a third of the distance between the Ram and us. Then I saw the big-looking black shot rising and coming straight towards where I was standing…The shot struck the water some forty to fifty feet away, dashing up a great quantity of water which came down on the after end of the Nahant in a torrent and wet me to the skin, and then I saw the shot go past, tumbling end over end upon the water, and making such a roaring as I imagine might be made by a small tornado. That "roar" in my ears, added to the ducking I had received, brought me to realize that I was where I had no business to be.[156]

The shot, though aimed at the *Weehawken*, had passed over the stern of its intended target, streaked past the *Nahant*'s pilothouse and splashed into the sound, throwing up a geyser of water alongside the ship. Another flash exploded from the muzzle of the *Atlanta*'s bow gun, but this shot, too, went wild, striking nothing but the water. Then Webb's starboard gun crew fired—with the same disappointing result. The Confederate ironclad's gun ports were so narrow that the cannons could only turn a few inches side to side; without the ability to move the ship itself, aiming directly at the enemy monitors was impossible. The *Atlanta* was helpless—it could neither fight nor escape.[157]

Now it was the *Weehawken*'s turn to fire—with murderous effect. At 5:15, as the monitor closed to within three hundred yards, Captain Rodgers ordered both of the cannons inside his rotating turret to be fired simultaneously. The shot from the smaller, eleven-inch-diameter gun passed harmlessly over the target, but the solid, four-hundred-pound ball from the larger, fifteen-inch smoothbore smashed into the starboard side of the *Atlanta*'s casemate about three feet behind the pilothouse, shattering its eighteen-inch-thick wooden backing and sending deadly shrapnel flying through the interior of the ship. A *Harper's Weekly* correspondent reported "that first shot virtually decided the action, for the terrible missile tore through her thick iron plating, backed by…solid timber, as if it were stubble, and prostrated about forty of her crew, some by splinters, but the most part by the mere concussion, without being personally touched." Commander Webb confirmed that at least thirty men were incapacitated by that first shot—some seriously injured, others simply stunned by the concussion of the blast.[158]

As the *Nahant* moved forward to join its sister ship in pummeling the helpless Confederate ironclad, the *Weehawken*'s two guns opened up again, and both projectiles hit their mark, though with disparate effects. First came one of the *Weehawken*'s eleven-inch cannonballs. It smacked into the *Atlanta*'s "knuckle"—the angled edge of the armored deck where the iron wrapped around the sides of the hull and projected down into the water. Aside from denting the metal and dislodging a plate or two, no serious harm was done. Then the massive fifteen-inch gun belched smoke and fire for a second time, exacting a terrible toll on the adversary. This time, the heavy ball smashed into the armored roof of the *Atlanta*'s pilothouse, "crushing it like latticework," in the words of the *Atlanta*'s surgeon, Dr. Robert Gibbes, and severely injuring the two men standing inside the structure. Now another eleven-inch shell slammed into the *Atlanta*, striking dead center of the heavy iron shutter that hung over one of the starboard gun ports. The force of the collision broke the shutter clean in two and sent a jagged fragment hurtling through the interior of the casemate, dealing destruction among the unfortunate men

The pilothouse of the CSS *Atlanta* (foreground) is shattered by a solid shot from the fifteen-inch cannon of the monitor USS *Weehawken*. *Hargrett Rare Book & Manuscript Library, University of Georgia.*

working the gun on the other side of the wall. It was, in the words of surgeon Gibbes, "a microcosm of human suffering, pain, and confusion."[159]

Throughout this terrible ordeal, as *Weehawken*'s four solid cannonballs hammered the sides and top of the stranded Confederate ironclad, the *Atlanta*'s uninjured crew members had stood bravely by their guns, managing to lob a total of seven iron bolts—a type of shot flattened at the end to enable it to deliver a hefty punch against metal armor—at the oncoming monitor. But because their ship was immobile and it was impossible to correctly aim any of the guns, none of the shots managed to strike the *Weehawken* or the *Nahant*. Describing Webb's predicament, James D. Bulloch wrote, "It can hardly be said that he was fighting his ship—he was simply enduring the fire of his adversary."[160] To Webb, it was clear that the only way to prevent more carnage among his crew was to surrender his vessel. At 5:30 a.m., he ordered the *Atlanta*'s massive Confederate flag to be lowered and a white flag raised in its place. The *Nahant*, which had held fire until it was closer in, had just caught up with the *Weehawken*. Seeing the *Atlanta* strike its colors, the *Nahant*'s captain, Commander John Dodwnes, reversed his ship's engines. It was too late to stop the onrushing monitor, which thudded up against the *Atlanta*'s armored knuckle before gliding to a stop. Webb, fearing that this naval fender-bender might mean his adversaries were unaware he had given up the fight, rushed outside onto the exposed deck and shouted, "I surrender!" The mightiest warship in the Confederate navy had been brought to its knees in thirty-five minutes.[161]

Recalling the grim determination of the *Atlanta*'s crew, Carpenter's Mate George W. Hardcastle remembered, "It was impossible to get the men from their guns to look after them (the wounded), until Capt. Webb said to his men, 'I have given up the ship.'" Paymaster's Clerk John W. Carey insisted: "We were not ashamed of it, for we were aground and at the enemy's mercy, the shots which they fired going right through our ship. It would have been murder to have continued the action, for every man on board would have been killed." Seaman W.B. Moore added, "Every man stood nobly at his post from the first to last."[162] According to a report in one Northern newspaper, Commander Webb delivered a pained but eloquent speech to his crestfallen crew:

> *I have surrendered our vessel because circumstances over which I had no control, have compelled me to do so. I know that you started upon this expedition with high hopes, and you have been disappointed. I most earnestly wish it had happened otherwise but Providence, for some good reason, has interfered with our plans, and we have failed of success. You all know that if we had not run aground the result would have been different, and now that a regard for your lives has influenced me in this surrender, I would advise you to submit quietly to the fate which has overtaken us. I hope that we may all soon be returned to our homes and meet again in a common brotherhood.*[163]

At the completion of this short soliloquy, reported the *Philadelphia Inquirer*, Webb was so overcome that he fainted. While it seems reasonable to assume that the unexpectedly defeated officer spoke at least a few emotionally charged words to his men, it is unlikely that Webb swooned at the culmination of his address. The *Inquirer* article is the only mention in any published report—media, government or personal—of Webb's speech, and likewise there are no other stories about him losing consciousness.

Aboard the gunboats CSS *Isondiga* and CSS *Resolute* farther up the sound, Webb's Confederate colleagues stared in disbelief as the *Atlanta*'s big Confederate flag was lowered to the deck and Webb surrendered the vessel. It was clear something had gone wrong around the time the ironclad began firing. Webb's secretary, C. Lucian Jones, who observed the fighting from the deck of the *Resolute*, reported, "The *Atlanta* did not appear to move after she first grounded. It seemed as if the *Atlanta* was captured in the very place she grounded."[164] The startled crews of the two wooden-hulled ships had little time to take in the unexpected turn of events, for Captain Rodgers sent the gunboat USS *Cimarron*, the U.S. Navy blockading vessel normally on station on Wassaw Sound, up the sound to capture or engage the Confederate vessels. Lacking the protection of their now-surrendered ironclad guardian, the Southern ships raised steam and retreated up the Wilmington River to safety. It was far from the ending their commanders had envisioned for the mission.[165] Aboard the *Nahant*, Commander Downes, who was still smarting at the fact that he'd not gotten off a single shot at the *Atlanta* before it suddenly surrendered, vented his frustration at the departing Confederate gunboats. "Oh you Secesh devils," he cried out, "you came to see us threshed did you. & be d—d! Now go back where you belong." U.S. Navy surgeon Charles Ellery Stedman, who witnessed the scene, chuckled, "It was very absurd, considering that the fellows were 3 miles off."[166] Commander Downes and other Union officers present mistakenly believed that the Confederate gunboats carried civilian spectators who had come to watch the *Atlanta* defeat the Union monitors. However, no Confederate sources—official or otherwise—support this contention.[167]

As soon as the fighting had stopped, Webb dispatched his second-in-command, Lieutenant J.W. Alexander, to the *Weehawken* to formally surrender the *Atlanta*. Shortly afterward, when a small boat full of Union officers rowed over from the *Nahant*, Webb tried to hand over his own sword, as a token of surrender, to the *Nahant*'s executive officer, Lieutenant Commander David Harmony, whom Webb had known when both served in the old navy before the war. Harmony declined the sword, insisting Webb surrender it in person to the *Weehawken*'s Captain Rodgers, who was the senior Union officer present. As it turned out, Rodgers allowed Webb and his officers to keep their swords, and he even ordered the victorious Union sailors not to cheer, in order to spare the *Atlanta*'s crew any embarrassment. "Poor devils, they feel badly enough without our cheering," he wrote shortly afterward, adding, "There had not been time to get up any blood or become in the least savage, and when I saw the white flag…I only felt sorry for our prisoners."[168]

Though he permitted Webb to keep his sword, Lieutenant Commander Harmony did subject the Confederates to the indignity of seeing the Stars and Stripes raised over their shattered ship.[169] Inside the *Atlanta*'s casemate, the gun deck was cluttered with debris and echoed with the cries of injured men. Hardcastle reported, "The ship, at the time of the surrender, was in an awful condition…inside, the woodwork was driven off from the iron plates to the diameter of eight or ten feet, and the gun deck piled up with the rubbish. The wounded were lying on all sides."[170] Surgeon Charles Ellery Stedman from the *Nahant* was sent over to the *Atlanta* to help care for the suffering sailors. He wrote later, "We amputated one arm & another leg was needing [to be amputated]."[171] In all, sixteen of the *Atlanta*'s sailors were wounded badly enough to require hospitalization after the battle. Another, Orderly Sergeant Littleton Barrett, died two hours later of his injuries. Barrett, a Methodist minister from northeast Georgia, had joined the *Atlanta*'s crew just a few days before the engagement.[172]

When the surrender formalities were completed and the wounded were under the surgeon's care, the *Atlanta*'s officers were split between the *Nahant* and *Weehawken*—roughly ten to each ship—and treated to breakfast with their captors. While the Yankee sailors were embarrassed at the rough fare they had to offer their defeated Southern guests, the meal was actually quite a treat for the Confederates—circumstances notwithstanding—who were used to meager meals as a result of the Union blockade. The *Nahant*'s ship's boy, Alvah Folsom Hunter, remembered:

> *We had not been in touch with a supply steamer for two weeks or more and some stores were low. We boys felt that we hadn't a very good breakfast to offer our guests, but one of the Confederate mid-shipmen, a young chap about my own age with whom I had a considerable chat, told me it was the best breakfast he had eaten in some time, and that the coffee served to them at our mess table was the first "sure-enough coffee" he had tasted in six months.*[173]

Surgeon Stedman, who sat down to eat after the U.S. steamer *Island City* came to evacuate the wounded Confederate sailors to Fort Pulaski, wrote, "The Capt. Appeared to be a nice fellow, but the 1st & 2nd lieutenants were very drunk by noontime."[174] The *Philadelphia Inquirer* correspondent who wrote about Webb's alleged swooning surrender speech also provided a less-than-sterling description of the commander's men:

> *One cannot imagine a more villainous-looking set of men than this same "Atlanta" crew. They are all Georgia "crackers," the poorest "white trash" of Georgia, without education, or anything, in fact, which would*

entitle them to be called men, except that they have the human form. Not one man among them is a sailor, but they are all soldiers. The officers being perfect gentlemen, compared strangely with this gang of cutthroats…a more dejected looking set of naval heroes never trod the deck of our gun-boat before.[175]

At 8:30 a.m., the *Weehawken*'s acting first assistant engineer, J.G. Young, reversed the *Atlanta*'s engines and, with the tide higher than it had been during the battle, managed to pull the stranded Confederate ironclad free of the stubborn mud and sand.[176] With a prize crew in charge and the American flag flying overhead, the battered warship steamed north to Port Royal. Though total numbers in after-action reports vary, just under 150 members of the *Atlanta*'s crew, including more than 20 officers, were now prisoners of the U.S. military.[177]

In Savannah, news of the *Atlanta*'s surrender was greeted with shock and disbelief. "Our community was startled yesterday morning by the report," wrote the editor of the *Savannah Daily Morning News*, promising as soon as possible "to obtain fuller information in regard to this most mortifying and disastrous affair."[178] With no firsthand knowledge of what took place aboard the defeated ironclad, and in spite of the appearance that the ship had run aground, many Savannahians gave credence to conspiracy theories and cast blame on the *Atlanta*'s enlisted crew. An anonymous editorialist hissed in the *Morning News* the next day, "My opinion is that the *Atlanta* has been betrayed to the enemy by base treachery."[179] Lieutenant Joel S. Kennard, who witnessed the battle from a distance aboard the *Isondiga*, lent credibility to these dark rumors when he wrote in his official report:

The cause of Webb's surrender can, of course, only be a matter of conjecture, but it is unreasonable to suppose that one who could conceive and attempt so daring a scheme would have so soon struck his colors without some cause entirely beyond his control; such, for instance, as the entire loss of locomotion, or, which I think more probably, the mutiny of his crew.[180]

The crew's honor was restored when, ten days after the battle, letters arrived from the prison ship USS *Vermont* in Port Royal Harbor, where the *Atlanta*'s enlisted sailors and marines were being held. In the letters, the men related the truth about their actions in the battle and about how the *Atlanta*'s grounding had prevented the ship from fighting or escaping. "It shows that the *Atlanta* surrendered simply because she was unfit for such a fight, having been so seriously damaged by their shot that a continuance of the struggle would have resulted in her utter destruction, with all on board," declared James Roddy Sneed, editor of the *Savannah Republican*, who had been more reluctant than his competitor at the *Morning News* to blame the crew. Sneed closed with a swipe at his opponent, crowing, "This is just as we expected and shows how cautious we should be in inferring treason against brave Southern men. We hope the *News* and its correspondents will learn a lesson from this experience, and cease to indulge in unjust and horrible suspicions about their countrymen for the future."[181] Following his eventual release from a Northern prison and exchange later in the war, Commander Webb himself vindicated the conduct of his men, writing, "I can not speak too highly of the officers and crew under my command. They all displayed those qualities which are inherent in brave men, combining coolness with perfect obedience, though the majority of the crew were from the mountains of Georgia and had but a limited idea of a ship of war."[182]

Captain John Rodgers, the ranking U.S. Navy officer in the battle, received special written thanks from Congress and President Lincoln and was promoted to commodore.[183] Most of the *Atlanta*'s enlisted crew members were paroled and returned to Savannah within a few weeks of their capture. For Commander Webb and his officers, the end of the short battle represented the beginning of a long period of confinement as prisoners of war in Northern jails—first Fort Lafayette in New York, then Fort Warren in Boston.[184] Their confinement ended in the fall of 1864, when the men were exchanged for an equal number of Union prisoners held in the South. Webb was briefly assigned command of the ironclad CSS *Richmond* in Virginia, but he resigned his commission before the end of the year, citing health reasons.[185]

After steaming to Port Royal under her own power, the *Atlanta* was anchored in the midst of its former foes. Perhaps the once-mighty Confederate ironclad was never as fearsome as Union commanders believed. Alvah Folsom Hunter wrote about what he saw when he toured the surrendered Southern ship during his day off on Sunday, July 5, 1863:

> *We were much surprised to find her in such a half-finished condition inside. The entire casemate deck was open from end to end, with only unbleached muslin partitions separating the quarters of the crew from the officers wardroom aft, and there had manifestly been much haste in getting her ready for service....*

The spar-torpedo-arm on the bow was manifestly a crude apparatus, and the elbow-like arrangement for lowering the spar into the water was a decidedly clumsy affair. A line from the trigger in the base of the torpedo was passed through three or four small staples set along the top of the spar and on into the box port, and a sharp pull upon this lanyard was to explode the torpedo at the right moment—if everything went just right! Whether such a clumsy apparatus could be successfully worked in the exciting moment of contact with an enemy vessel could only be told by trying, but that spar-torpedo certainly didn't look to be very dangerous to us after we had examined it carefully.[186]

Later, the *Atlanta* was towed to the navy yard in Philadelphia. Here it was exhibited for a time as a fundraiser for the Union Volunteer Refreshment Saloon, a citizen-staffed nonprofit organization that provided aid for more than 800,000 Union troops passing in and out of the city during the war.[187] A prize court condemned the *Atlanta* and awarded all crew members from the U.S. Navy vessels present at her capture—USS *Weehawken*, USS *Nahant* and USS *Cimarron*—shares of the prize money proportional to their rank. The

The ex–CSS *Atlanta*, rechristened USS *Atlanta*, on patrol with the Federal fleet in the James River, Virginia, in 1864 or 1865. *Naval History and Heritage Command.*

Above: The author poses, for scale, beside the CSS *Atlanta*'s massive, sixteen-foot-by-twenty-four-foot flag at the National Civil War Naval Museum in Columbus, Georgia. *Photo by Jeff Josefsberg.*

Right: The CSS *Atlanta*'s four rifled cannons are exhibited at the National Museum of the U.S. Navy at the Washington Navy Yard. *Photo courtesy of Craig Swain/ To the Sound of the Guns blog*

Atlanta and its contents were appraised at $350,829.26.[188] As ship's boy on the *Nahant*, Hunter was entitled to $176.16. Hunter's check arrived in June 1864, when the young man was serving as a soldier in the U.S. Army Signal Corps in Mississippi.[189]

Repaired, re-armed and commissioned USS *Atlanta* in February 1864 (perhaps it was considered more insulting to keep the name and simply change the "C" to a "U"), the former Confederate ironclad served as part of the U.S. Navy's blockading force in the James River downstream from the Confederate capital of Richmond, Virginia.[190] After the war, the *Atlanta* was decommissioned and laid up for a few years, then sold to the government of Haiti, which was embroiled in its own civil war and needed naval vessels. Renamed *Triumph*, the ex-*Fingal*, ex–CSS *Atlanta* and ex–USS *Atlanta* was last seen in Lewes, Delaware, at 4:15 p.m. on December 17, 1869. Commanded by a Haitian admiral, it carried several former U.S. Navy officers—presumably working as advisors to the Haitians—and was crewed by a group of mostly African American sailors hired at the docks in Philadelphia. After departing the Delaware capes and sailing into the teeth of the storm, the ship was never heard from again and is presumed to have sunk—not surprising in light of the vessel's well-known leakiness and general unseaworthiness when it sailed as the CSS *Atlanta*. More than 120 people were aboard when it vanished.[191]

While the *Atlanta* itself is lost to history, tangible reminders of the June 17, 1863 Battle of Wassaw Sound remain today. The warship's four original rifled cannons are on exhibit out-of-doors at the National Museum of the United States Navy, located inside the Washington Navy Yard in Washington, D.C. The guns were removed and replaced with larger weapons when the *Atlanta* was reborn as a Union warship. Each of the captured cannons is inscribed with text identifying its caliber (barrel and projectile size) along with the date and details of its capture.

At a casual glance, the bluish-gray gun tubes could easily be mistaken for other, less-noteworthy Civil War cannons, but another artifact of the CSS *Atlanta* displayed at a museum 750 miles away truly stands out. When visitors walk into the gallery of the National Civil War Naval Museum in Columbus, Georgia, their eyes are invariably drawn to the massive, sixteen-by-twenty-four-foot Confederate flag hanging on the wall—the same standard that floated over the ill-fated *Atlanta* during its final hours as a Confederate warship. Many other Civil War flags and naval ensigns adorn the walls of the museum, but all are dwarfed by the *Atlanta*'s—a solid white rectangle with the familiar Confederate battle flag in its upper-left-hand corner.[192] In the century and a half since the ship itself slipped beneath the waves of the Atlantic Ocean, this span of barely faded cloth has come to serve as a reminder of the hopes and dreams that were crushed when the proud banner was lowered in surrender one late-spring morning in 1863.

Prisoners by the Park

Savannah's First "Yankee Tourists"

This is truly the oasis in the desert of our prison lives.
—*Captain Willard Glazier, Second New York Cavalry Regiment*

Modern-day Savannah is known worldwide as the "Hostess City of the South," welcoming more than thirteen million tourists each year.[193] Coincidentally, many of those visitors hail from states north of the Mason-Dixon line. In late 1864, Savannah hosted several thousand men from some of those same states—but in this instance, the city's hospitality got decidedly mixed reviews.

On July 28 of that year, readers of the *Savannah Daily Morning News* were probably unsettled to learn that "twelve hundred Yankee officers are to be removed to Savannah," because "Macon is overflowed with sick and wounded." Confederate authorities were forced to move Union prisoners of war to other parts of the state—though the true reason for moving the prisoners was to place them out of reach of Union cavalry raids in the Macon area.[194] In the end, only about six hundred enemy officers were transported to Savannah from mid-Georgia, but their arrival still caused quite a stir.[195] John Vestal Hadley of Indiana later described the scene that unfolded when he and his fellow prisoners disembarked their train and walked east on Liberty Street on July 30. "As we were the first Yankees, armed or disarmed, ever in the city, the citizens manifested a great curiosity to see us," Hadley remembered. "Everybody was out to see the Yankees. The street through which we had to pass…was literally walled on either side with old men, women, and children, of all colors." When an angry young Confederate woman brazenly waved her "Bonnie Blue Flag" in the Union officers' faces, one saucy Yank suggested she use it to patch a hole in the seat of his uniform pants. We can only imagine how this Southern belle received the suggestion.[196]

The Union officers were interned within a roughly two-acre stockade on the grounds of the Marine Hospital on the southeastern outskirts of the city (the structure still stands along Drayton Street on the northeastern edge of Forsyth Park and is today known as the old Candler Hospital). The hastily erected prison was christened Camp Davidson, in honor of its first commandant, a Confederate officer named H.H. Davison.[197] To create the enclosure, Confederate authorities fastened four-foot-long wooden boards, standing upright, atop the three preexisting eight-foot-tall brick walls surrounding the hospital. A new fourth wall was constructed entirely of wood. Sentry boxes overlooked the enclosure.[198] The prisoners lived in tents laid out in an organized fashion, "so that the camp has quite a military appearance," according to one inmate.[199]

At night, the stockade was lit by fires burning atop five-foot-tall wooden stands. Though the flickering firelight allowed the guards to keep an eye on the prisoners' movements, it also offered some comfort to the confined men. "During the pleasant evenings it was not an uncommon occurrence to see groups of the officers sitting near these fires," remembered Lieutenant A.O. Abbott, "engaged in reading, studying, or playing games."[200] During the day, other fires burned within a number of brick ovens and beneath large iron pots and skillets. The prisoners were expected to bake their own cornbread, boil their own rice, fry their own meat and wash their own clothing.[201]

Though the ad hoc prison pen was far from luxurious, it was still a drastic improvement over Camp Oglethorpe, the rough, unsanitary facility where the captured officers had been locked up in Macon.[202] In a number of books written after the war, the Union officers described the Savannah camp in glowing terms. Captain Willard Glazier of New York gushed, "So great is the contrast between our treatment here and at other places, that we cannot but feel that fortune has certainly smiled kindly upon us for once.…This is truly the oasis in the desert of our prison lives."[203] Major Alfred E. Calhoun was even more blown away; describing his first impression of the place on the morning after his arrival, he wrote, "When we awoke in the morning, it was like a glimpse of Eden."[204]

The food distributed in this Eden may not have been heavenly by normal standards, but it far exceeded the prisoners' expectations. An astonished Abbott wrote:

> How exquisite was the taste of the crackers and molasses! It was the first wheat bread I had eaten since my entry into Richmond—nine months before—and molasses had been stranger to me for years. After the corn bread we had so long lived upon, this was manna. It seems that the Commissary at Savannah labored under the delusion that he must issue to us the same rations as were served out to the Rebel soldiers and sailors.[205]

Among the camp's most appreciated features were the trees that stood within its walls. "Quite a number of large, moss-covered live-oak trees are growing within the enclosure, which will furnish a refreshing shade from the oppressive noon-day sun," wrote Captain Glazier.[206] Lieutenant Alonzo Cooper described the prison yard as "quite well shaded with live oak trees, some of which grew to enormous dimensions, one on the south side, spreading over nearly or quite a hundred feet of ground."[207] Guards permitted the prisoners to climb up into the branches and enjoy the view of a town known locally as the "Forest City." A monument erected a few years before the war, honoring Revolutionary War hero Casimir Pulaski, protruded from the green canopy. "By climbing into the trees [fellow prisoner] Bell and myself had a good view of Savannah," wrote Calhoun, "with the fine Pulaski monument rising from a parallelogram of green in the centre."[208] Glazier concurred, writing, "Pulaski's monument stands within plain view. This is a fine structure, about forty feet in height."[209]

The prisoners uniformly gave high praise to their Confederate guards, who were members of the First Georgia Infantry Regiment, also known as the First Georgia Regulars. John Vestal Hadley of Indiana reported that the guards "treated us humanely and in marked contrast with the authorities at Macon. These were old soldiers and knew a soldier's lot, and how to sympathize with him as a prisoner."[210] Calhoun echoed Hadley's sentiments, describing the guards as "old soldiers, native Georgians, and I will add, with respectful emphasis, they were gentlemen."[211] Glazier surmised that shared combat experience bonded the Confederate guards and their Union charges, explaining, "there is nothing like the adventures of the battle-field and the mutual sufferings there experienced, to teach soldiers humanity towards each other.…These Georgia boys will be long remembered, and may look for the utmost kindness and consideration from us, if chance ever reverses our circumstances."[212]

Union officers imprisoned in Savannah in 1864 climbed trees to get a view of the Pulaski Monument in Monterrey Square, pictured here during a Confederate military parade. *Courtesy of Hugh Golson.*

Good treatment, sheltering trees and kind guards notwithstanding, the Yankee officers made numerous attempts to escape their captivity and reach Union-held Fort Pulaski, located fourteen miles to the east, whose morning and evening signal guns could be heard inside the stockade in Savannah.[213] Lieutenant Abbott remembered, "It was not long after our arrival here before the tunneling commenced."[214] "Tunnelling [*sic*], as a means of escape, has become quite an institution," wrote Glazier.[215] Both officers reported that two separate tunnels were being excavated simultaneously beneath the stockade walls. Abbott's tunneling escapade ended when a sharp-eyed sentinel saw the escaping prisoner's head pop up above the ground outside the stockade wall and cried out, "Go back dar, you Yank, or I will shoot."[216] Glazier's tunnel, which extended past the outside ring of sentinels, came to a more prosaic end:

> *The work was progressing finely when, in the afternoon, a cow, passing over the tunnel, broke through, and was unable to extricate herself. The*

Rebels, seeing her in difficulty, came to the rescue, and thus discovered our work….

That poor, stupid cow had brought to light by mere chance, what Rebel scrutiny had failed to discover. There were no blessings for the cow that day—at least, not within the stockade."[217]

One of the Confederate guards, First Sergeant W.H. Andrews, confirmed in his diary the story of the cow caving in the tunnel, noting that the wily Yankee prisoners "have to be watched very close to keep them from getting out." Still, Andrews added, "I don't blame them, would get out too if I was in the same condition and could get out….Hope I may never be a prisoner of war."[218] According to prisoner accounts, no Union officer successfully escaped from the stockade beside the hospital; one, a Captain Sampson of the Second Massachusetts Heavy Artillery, crawled through a hole beneath the wooden wall on the side of the stockade and slogged through salt marsh to within sight of Fort Pulaski before he was recaptured by a Confederate patrol.[219]

After spending roughly six weeks in Savannah, the Yankee officers were marched back to the train station and transported to Charleston on September 13, 1864, so that their guards could be freed up to serve in coastal artillery batteries in areas outside Savannah where Union forces had recently become active.[220] Unfortunately for the local Confederate commanders, however, events beyond their control were already bringing an even larger group of Union prisoners into the city. Union general William T. Sherman had taken the city of Atlanta, and Confederate commanders feared their unpredictable adversary might make a move to liberate the thousands of Union enlisted troops imprisoned in the notorious stockade at Andersonville, Georgia. Consequently, the prison authorities scrambled to move the POWs to other parts of the Confederacy.

In Savannah, Confederate general Lafayette McLaws was shocked to receive news on September 7, 1864, that the first batch of inmates from Andersonville would arrive in Savannah the very next day. He instructed Colonel Edward C. Anderson, who was by this time in command of Confederate artillery in the fortifications surrounding the city, immediately to begin work on a new, larger stockade behind the Chatham County Jail. This facility was located at the southwest corner of Hall and Whitaker Streets, adjacent to Forsyth Park but across the park from the officers' stockade at the hospital. As predicted, nine hundred Yankee soldiers arrived on September 8.[221] An irate McLaws dashed off an angry note to his higher-ups, complaining that his forces were already stretched too thin to defend the coast against the Union troops on their doorstep, much less to guard Union prisoners. "I have not now a single man in reserve to support any point that may be threatened by the enemy," he griped.[222] But McLaws's cries fell on deaf ears, for by early October, the new stockade behind the jail was crowded with more than seven thousand Union troops.[223]

By all accounts, the pitiful collection of humanity that arrived on Savannah's doorstep in the fall of 1864 was a shock to the citizens of the war-weary city, eliciting reactions of simultaneous pity and disgust. Charles C. Jones described the men as "the most miserable, degraded, ragged, filthy wretches your eyes ever beheld."[224] Colonel Anderson added, "They were dirty and half clad and altogether the most squalid gathering of humanity it has ever been my lot to look upon."[225] Though they were hungry and suffering themselves due to the Union blockade and the sinking fortunes of the Confederacy, Savannah civilians crowded around the stockade on September 9, 10 and 11, making attempts to relieve the prisoners' suffering. "Among them I noticed a large number of respectably-dressed women," wrote Anderson, "some of whom were throwing bread to the Yankees."[226] First Sergeant Andrews, the Confederate guard from the officers' stockade outside the hospital, witnessed the spectacle and observed, "There must have been between 500 and 1,000 women and children visited [sic] the stockade carrying baskets of provisions. They became so numerous, the guard could not keep them back….If the prisoners had made a break, would have had to of [sic] fired among the women and children or let the prisoners escape."[227]

The exact dimensions of the new enlisted men's stockade are unknown, but its construction was similar to that of the officers' prison across the park, though without the preexisting brick walls at the base. First Sergeant Andrews wrote, "The stockade is built of plank set up and down and about 12 feet high with sentry boxes at proper intervals to overlook the prison."[228] A drawing by prisoner Robert K. Sneden shows locomotive headlamps hung on the walls to provide illumination at night. The color sketch depicts a sprawling tent city within the high wooden palisade.[229] Sneden wrote, "The whole camp has the appearance of a village of dog kennels. All are cooking, and fires are kept up all night, at which the ragged and shoeless prisoners sit, eating and smoking until midnight."[230] German immigrant Frederick Emil Schmitt, captured while serving in a New Jersey regiment, wrote derisively, "This camp was as level as a pancake, consisted of nothing but sand, and was as hot as an oven. It was no fit place for human beings, but especially no place for sick people."[231] Another conspicuous difference between the officer and enlisted stockades was the absence of big oak trees in the newer enclosure. Even Colonel Anderson, the man who built the compound, admitted, "The stockade is entirely without shelter and the burning sun bakes down upon them from daylight till dark."[232] Savannah's torrential rains could cause the prisoners to suffer even more than its searing sun. "We had this morning before daylight one of the heaviest thunderstorms that I have known for years," Anderson wrote in his diary on October 3. "The rain poured down in torrents. I thought of the poor prisoners confined on our outskirts and pitied them from the bottom of my heart. Think of nearly seven thousand men cooped up in a stockade without shelter."[233]

In spite of the lack of shelter, conditions in the Savannah stockade were better than what the Northern soldiers had endured in their previous prison. Illinois cavalryman John McElroy conceded, "After all Savannah was a wonderful improvement on Andersonville. We got away from the pestilential Swamp and that poisonous ground. Every mouthful of air was not laden with disease germs, nor every cup of water polluted with the seeds of death. The earth did not breed gangrene, nor the atmosphere promote fever."[234] Sergeant Daniel George Kelley of New York offered an equally positive assessment, reporting that rations were better in Savannah than at Andersonville, and in Savannah, the prisoners were allowed to see a doctor every three to four days.[235]

The enlisted prison stockade behind the Chatham County Jail housed approximately seven thousand Union soldiers for several weeks in late 1864. *Virginia Historical Society.*

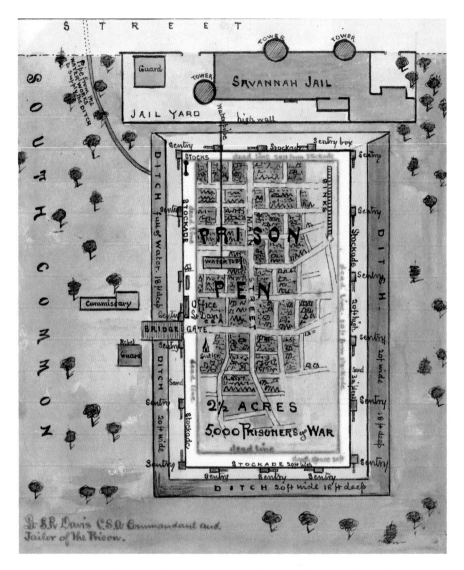

Confederate authorities dug a ditch around the stockade and filled the ditch with water to stop prisoners from tunneling under the wall. *Virginia Historical Society.*

Still, the temptation to dig their way out to freedom was too strong for many of the Union soldiers to resist. McElroy explained, "The Rebels, who knew nothing of our burrowing propensities, had neglected to make the plank forming the walls of the Prison project any distance below the surface of the ground…so that it looked as if everything was arranged expressly to invite us to tunnel out." The results were predictable. "When morning came it looked as if a colony of gigantic rats had been at work," McElroy declared.[236] In his diary, Colonel Anderson mentions two specific tunneling attempts, one of which was initially successful; additional attempts may have taken place.[237] The Confederate authorities employed various methods to prevent such escapes. McElroy reported that one technique involved driving a heavily laden mule-drawn cart around the inside of the stockade. "The wheels or the mule's feet broke through the thin sod covering the tunnels and exposed them," McElroy explained, adding, "This put an end to subterranean engineering."[238] The prisoners were effectively sealed up inside the stockade after Colonel Anderson ordered a gang of slaves to dig a ten-foot-wide, six-foot-deep ditch around the entire enclosure and fill it with water. This moat precluded any further attempts at tunneling to freedom.[239]

Many of the Union prisoners were already weakened and malnourished by the time they arrived in Savannah. Two days after the officers were sent away to Charleston, their former stockade beside the hospital was filled with between five and six hundred sick enlisted prisoners, many of whom were so ill they had to be ferried into the enclosure in wagons.[240] The first mention of prisoners dying appears in Colonel Anderson's diary on September 17, when he noted, "The mortality thus far has not been great. The dead are laid aside until near sundown or early in the morning, when they are carried off in a wagon accompanied by a burying detail of prisoners under guard and put into the ground without shroud or service." The Yankee corpses were placed into the ground along Ogeechee Road, just outside the ring of fortifications that guarded the city.[241] Anderson witnessed a perfunctory prisoner burial at the remote location. "They were lying cold and stark on the chilled earth whilst a party of prisoners under guard were digging a pit to inter them," he wrote. "On these occasions no service is held over the dead nor are the bodies coffined, but they are laid in one grave together and small mounds corresponding in number with the bodies entered are thrown up on the surface."[242]

Thirty-eight Union soldiers had been buried beside the road by September 25, an average of just over two deaths per day.[243] However, when the weather in Savannah turned suddenly and unexpectedly cold, conditions in the stockade took a deadly turn. "We all suffered a great deal from this cause, and many were chilled to death," wrote Sergeant Kelley.[244] Twenty-five prisoners died in a single night on October 9–10, and twenty-six more perished over the course of the following evening. When he visited the stockade that morning, Anderson was horrified by what he found. "It was a sickening sight to see those wretched strangers, stripped off stark and stiff in the death line awaiting transportation to their place of burial," he confided in his diary. "The flies were swarming over their faces and a crew of prisoners had gathered nearby looking on in callous indifference and jesting among themselves as though there had never existed a feeling of pity in their hearts."[245] In all, roughly one hundred enlisted Union prisoners perished during their stay in Savannah.[246] The pitiful condition of the prisoners weighed on the consciences of their guards. "How cruel to keep men in prison when they could be paroled and allowed to return home until exchanged," wrote First Sergeant Andrews. "But they have no one to blame but their own government, for the Confederacy would jump at the offer and be glad of the chance to get rid of them."[247]

Savannah was soon rid of its POW problem, for just four short weeks after the first enlisted prisoners arrived, a new, larger stockade named Camp Lawton opened eighty-five miles away in Millen, Georgia. Trains began ferrying prisoners to Millen on October 11, and all except four hundred of the sickest men were cleared out of Savannah by October 13.[248] Against Colonel Anderson's better judgement, General McLaws ordered the stockade behind the Chatham County Jail to be demolished. The general wanted to make sure Savannah could never again be forced to serve as a prison pen.[249]

THE BIG SKEDADDLE

The Confederate Evacuation of Savannah, December 1864

The rebels kept up a bold front till 2 o'clock last night, when they ignominiously skedaddled like [the] *thieves and scoundrels they are.*
—*Wesley De Haven, Sixteenth Wisconsin Infantry Regiment*

When General William Tecumseh Sherman set out on his now-famous "March to the Sea," leaving Atlanta on November 16, 1864, no one knew whether he would successfully reach his destination—or even what that destination was.[250] Even as Confederate forces failed time and again to slow Sherman's advance, the people of Savannah held out hope that their city would be spared. A Southern newspaper correspondent later wrote, "People were in the dark as to what was going on. They hoped we would be able to force Sherman to the coast, either to the right or to the left, and save the city."[251]

But it would have been foolish to rely on hope alone, and Savannah's Confederate commander, Major General William J. Hardee, known as "Old Reliable" for his previous battlefield successes and penchant for thorough training and preparation, began the difficult task of preparing Savannah for battle. The city boasted strong defenses against attack by sea or from nearby Fort Pulaski, which had fallen to Union forces in April 1862. Now Hardee was forced to create new defenses to protect against land attack from the west—the direction of Sherman's approach.

Hardee began moving troops and cannons to the outskirts of Savannah on November 20.[252] His engineers constructed a thirteen-mile-long line of earthen defensive works situated about two and a half miles west of the city. These consisted of dirt forts with cannon emplacements, rifle pits and trenches. Hardee also employed an ingeniously simple means of slowing the enemy: he made the land impassable. There were only five approaches into the city from the west, and Hardee obstructed all of them.[253] He also broke dams and rice dikes, flooding the low ground with three to six feet of water.[254] Hardee's troops took their positions inside the fortifications and trenches on December 7—the day before Sherman's army arrived.[255] However, as Marine Lieutenant Henry L. Graves wrote to his mother, "We had splendid positions but not the men to hold them…where I was stationed there were not a hundred men where there ought for successful resistance, to have been at least five hundred."[256]

Savannah's Confederate garrison was badly outnumbered—and largely outclassed—by Sherman's force. Sherman boasted more than sixty thousand battle-hardened veterans, while Hardee could muster only about ten thousand men, more than a third of whom were poorly trained reserves and state troops (derisively dismissed by Sherman as "a mongrel mass"). Furthermore, hundreds of Hardee's soldiers were stationed at critical seafront fortifications protecting Savannah from attack by other Union forces and could not be spared to defend against Sherman. To help fill the gaps, Savannah mayor Richard D. Arnold ordered all able-bodied men in the city to report for duty with the army, declaring, "The time has come when every male who can shoulder a musket can make himself useful in defending our hearths and homes."[257]

General Sherman's blue-clad hordes arrived on the outskirts of Savannah on December 8–9. "We are in sight of the promised land, after a pilgrimage of three hundred miles," wrote Brigadier General John White Geary, who commanded one of Sherman's divisions. The Federal army unleashed what one Confederate officer described as "an incessant cannonade" of thundering artillery fire, and the Southerners responded in kind.[258] "Almost every breeze bears the hostile blast of the trumpet, and the thunder of the enemy's guns answers loudly to the thunder of our own," Geary wrote. In his official report of his division's actions during the March to the Sea, Geary estimated the Confederates fired as many as three hundred shells at his position each day during the height of the siege.[259] After close to a month on the march, the Federal troops were itching to take the city. "We are drawing our lines pretty close," wrote Indiana soldier Theodore F. Upson on December 11, "and were it not for the water in the ditches and streams around the City no doubt we would try to take the works by assault. Of course, we would lose a good many by this, but our boys are impatient and ready to try it."[260] The Confederate troops on the other side of the lines made clear from the beginning that they would hotly contest any Union assault. Legendary Confederate sharpshooter and scout Berry Benson, who served in the trenches outside Savannah with a volunteer battalion from Augusta, South Carolina, reported that even the unit's surgeon shouldered a rifle and joined in firing at the Yankees, "thinking, I reckon, that a surgeon can take off arms and legs with bullets as well as with the knife and saw."[261]

On December 13, Sherman's troops overran the small Confederate garrison at Fort McAllister on the Great Ogeechee River, about fifteen miles south of the city.[262] With the fall of this isolated post, Sherman was able to link up with Union naval and army forces operating out of Port Royal/ Hilton Head, South Carolina, and replenish his supplies for the first time since leaving Atlanta a month earlier. Sherman also started digging serious fortifications around Savannah—in some cases, less than five hundred feet from Confederate positions—and moved heavy cannons from Port Royal and captured guns from Fort McAllister into position to blast away at the Confederate defenders.[263] General Geary boasted, "My troops are now engaged throwing up immense batteries from which we expect to commence the bombardment of the city on next Tuesday. Being in good shelling range we will soon knock it to pieces….I think success is certain."[264]

From this point forward, time was on Sherman's side, not Hardee's. "There must be twenty-five thousand citizens, men, women, and children, in Savannah, that must also be fed, and how he is to feed them beyond a few days I cannot imagine," Sherman wrote to his commanding officer, Lieutenant General Ulysses S. Grant, on December 16. Sherman's goal was to pressure Hardee into surrendering Savannah, but Sherman intimated that he had no desire to "risk the lives of our men by assaults across the narrow causeways" leading into the city. If need be, Sherman averred, he would starve Hardee out, for, as he later wrote, "I had set my heart on the capture of Savannah."[265]

Hardee made clear to his superiors that he stood no chance of defending Savannah against Sherman with the forces under his command. He wrote to President Davis on December 15 that, unless significant reinforcements were sent, "I shall be compelled to evacuate Savannah." Two days later, Davis replied that no reinforcements could be spared and instructed Hardee to take whatever action was necessary "for the preservation of your army."[266] Hardee's immediate superior, General P.G.T. Beauregard, had been even more direct on December 8, two days before Sherman's arrival, when he wrote to Hardee, "Your forces being essential to the defense of Georgia and South Carolina, whenever you shall have to select between their safety and that of Savannah, sacrifice the latter." After visiting Savannah in person the next day to see the defenses firsthand, Beauregard instructed Hardee, "Should you have to decide between a sacrifice of the garrison or city, you will preserve the garrison for operations elsewhere."[267] Savannah was a lost cause, and the army was desperately needed to bolster General Lee's thinly stretched forces in Virginia.

Sherman officially demanded the surrender of Savannah on December 17, and Hardee refused the request the next day. However, the Confederates had begun working on a plan of escape a full day before Sherman's demand was received. At a late-night council of war on December 16, Hardee ordered General P.M.B. Young to immediately round up all of the rice flats he could find. These common wooden barges were used to transport rice and slaves on the canals crisscrossing the low country plantations.[268] Connected to stretch across the Savannah River, they could be used to form a temporary floating bridge out of the city.

Using steamboats, Young's troops collected thirty-one flats from area waterways—not enough to stretch across the river side by side, but sufficient to cover the distance if the flats were placed end to end. Each wooden barge was seventy-five to eighty feet long and just wide enough for a wagon to be safely pulled across. Working around the clock, ten Confederate navy sailors and a detachment of fifty-five Georgia state militia troops lashed the flats together with ropes and secured them with wooden stringers (boards nailed over the gaps between vessels to hold the barges together). Heavy metal wheels from railroad cars were used as makeshift anchors, and wooden planks torn from the city's wharves were repurposed as flooring atop the flats. For good measure, the builders spread straw atop the floating bridge to muffle the sound of troops marching across.[269]

The bridge was built in three sections. The first and largest section stretched roughly one thousand feet from the foot of West Broad Street (present-day Martin Luther King Jr. Boulevard) across the Savannah River to Hutchinson Island. A second, shorter bridge connected Hutchinson to Pennyworth Island. A third section bridged the gap between Pennyworth and the South Carolina shore. Hardee's engineers finished the first section by 8:00 p.m. on December 17, but heavy fog slowed their subsequent work, delaying completion of the remaining two bridges until 8:30 p.m. on December 19.[270] The evacuation could not begin until December 20 at the earliest.

Hardee circulated secret orders explaining the order of retreat: the light (portable) artillery would cross the bridge first, pulling their cannons by hand to keep their movements quiet. The bulk of the large force manning the city's western defenses would come next, with the troops stationed farthest from the city moving out first. Other troops, including the soldiers stationed at Fort Jackson and nearby fortifications, were to be evacuated by boat after sabotaging their weapons and throwing their ammunition into the river so the enemy would not be able to use it.[271]

Though Savannah's civilians certainly saw the floating bridge under construction and must have known what was about to happen, many seemed to be in a state of denial. After the city's fall, one man wrote:

Everybody was in a state of suspense. There was a pretty general hope that the city would be saved, but no one could give any substantial reason for this hope, having no certain grounds upon which to base it, and ignorance of the real condition kept them from arriving at a different conclusion and preparing for the worst.

All was uncertainty and doubt. Hope was mingled with fear, and it was difficult for any one [sic] to decide which preponderated in his own mind.... All were the victims of every imaginable kind—rumor and opinion, from the best to the worst. I hope never to pass through such dreadful days again. Such suspense is worse agony than reality, be it ever so dreadful.[272]

The sun set at 5:27 p.m. on Tuesday, December 20, allowing the first Confederate troops to creep quietly out of their trenches on the western outskirts of town.[273] For the next nine and a half hours, a long gray line of soldiers silently slithered over the floating bridges onto Hutchinson and Pennyworth Islands and thence to the South Carolina shore. Forty-nine pieces of light artillery rolled across first, followed by the horse-drawn wagons that carried their ammunition and supplies. The silent march was accompanied by the thunder of Confederate cannons firing at enemy positions. The Confederate artillery fire was heavier and more rapid than normal, as the cannoneers simultaneously covered the retreat and expended their remaining ammunition. "So, pretty much all day we were sending shells and solid shot across the rice field and broomstraw field beyond, into the pine forest where the enemy were camped," wrote Berry Benson. "It was very interesting to hear the cannonballs strike amongst the trees glancing from one to another, maybe striking four or five before falling to the ground."[274] The firing was kept up until the last possible

moment, when it was necessary for the crews to disable the heavy guns. A North Carolina Confederate band even struck up a performance of "Dixie"—to which the Union troops in the opposing trench responded by shouting, "Played out! Played out!"[275]

For the next nine and a half hours, unit after unit joined the sad procession, and participants left behind many evocative descriptions of the experience. Marine Lieutenant Henry Graves wrote to his mother:

I have no words to picture the gloomy bitterness that filled my breast on that dreary march through water, mud and darkness. Independent of the various feelings of a soldier turning his back on an enemy, of a Georgian abandoning his native State, of a patriot witnessing a disaster to his country's cause, and last but not least, of the instincts of humanity thinking of the certain and terrible suffering entailed on thousands in that devoted city, independent I say of all these, there pressed upon me the consciousness that some of the best and truest friends I have on earth were about to be abandoned in their utter helplessness to the power of an enemy.[276]

Like other members of his artillery command, Captain Cornelius Hanleiter of Atlanta had brought his wife and children to live in Savannah when he was assigned to the city. Now he was forced to evacuate without a chance to say goodbye. The spouses and children had gathered for safety at Bethesda Orphanage, near the location of the battery where their husbands and fathers were stationed. Hanleiter destroyed his unit's ammunition and

Savannah's ten thousand Confederate soldiers, sailors and marines walked across the Savannah River into South Carolina overnight on December 20–21, 1864, escaping William T. Sherman's encircling Union army. *Author's collection.*

disabled the guns, sending to the orphanage a large amount of food and bedding too cumbersome for the troops to carry. At this point, Hanleiter turned his back, placed his family's fate and his own in God's hands and began his long march out of Savannah. He confided to his diary:

I commenced to cross the first pontoon soon after ten o'clock. The night was exceedingly dark, and everything seemed to move on without system or direction. In the city, as we passed through, men were discharging their firearms, and making [the] night hideous with their oaths and blasphemies; horsemen were galloping about apparently without object, and women (maybe nymphs of the pavé) [an obsolete euphemism for prostitutes] going hither and thither. By the roadside and alongside of the pontoons, all night long, men and horses were strewn in confusion—some struggling in the mud and water, others, worn down with fatigue and perhaps sick of heart and in body, resting or asleep. These scenes were horrible in the extreme, and added no little to the disturbed condition of my mind. Several times during the march across Hutchinson's Island did I find myself endeavoring to render assistance to some poor fellow, or horse, that seemed to have been abandoned to his fate on the roadside, but each time hurried forward by the apparently endless mass of men and horses and mules and wagons and artillery behind me. Several wagons and teams and drivers were precipitated from the various bridges and lost or drowned, during the night—yet scarcely a word of sympathy was heard for either!

Captain Woodbury Wheeler, a veteran North Carolina officer, wrote:

It was about 11 o'clock when we silently marched down the City road, lined by the great live oak trees, with their long festoons of waving moss and vines which swung backward and forward, in the pale moonlight, and seemed to be ghosts of our departed hopes. We passed through the city and just as the clocks in the steeples struck "one!" our command had reached the centre of the dikes in the rice fields, which border the Carolina side of the Savannah River.[277]

For Berry Benson, the soundtrack of the evacuation was more rhythmic. "We were amongst the last to pass through, for the cavalry were going thro' at the same time," he remembered, "and it was a musical sound, in the dead of night, to hear the 'clink-clank, clink-clank' of the horses' iron feet as the troopers rode down the brick pavements."[278]

As he stepped off the pontoon bridge toward an uncertain future, John Barnwell Elliott, son of Bishop Stephen Elliott, reflected, "It seemed like an immense funeral procession stealing out of the city in the dead of night."[279] Elliott's father, the presiding bishop of the Confederate Episcopal Church, was one of an unknown number of civilians who joined the procession out of the abandoned city that night. A Confederate soldier noted, "Here and there could be seen a carriage whose owner had been fortunate enough to secure a passport."[280] Union general Ezra Carman looked down on the civilian exodus from his perch at a plantation on the South Carolina side of the river. "From the loft of a barn on my line I could see wagons, family carriages, men and women on foot, singly and in groups, moving north along the road," Carman observed. "Hardee had finished his pontoon-bridge, and the non-combatants were leaving the city....The stream of fugitives and the number of carriages and wagons increased as the day wore on."[281] Included in this number were James Roddy Sneed and William Tappan Thompson, editors of Savannah's two competing daily newspapers, the *Republican* and the *Daily Morning News*, respectively. Sneed managed to publish a final issue before his departure, imparting the following advice to frightened Savannahians in his last editorial:

To the Citizens of Savannah: By the fortunes of war we pass today under the authority of the Federal military forces. The evacuation of Savannah by the Confederate army, which took place last night, left the gates to the city open, and Sherman, with his army will, no doubt, to-day take possession....

This image clearly depicts the jumble of men, wagons and horses on the temporary floating bridge across the river. *Coastal Heritage Society, Savannah.*

> *It behooves all to keep within their homes until Gen. Sherman shall have organized a provost system and such police as will insure safety in persons as well as property. Let our conduct be such as to win the admiration of a magnanimous foe, and give no ground for complaint or harsh treatment on the part of him who will for an indefinite period hold possession of our city.*[282]

Throughout the night, Sherman's officers became increasingly alarmed by the possibility that the Confederate army might escape. General Geary discovered the existence of Hardee's pontoon bridge on the morning of December 20 and reported, "During the night I heard the movement of troops and wagons across the pontoon bridge."[283] General Carman had a front-row seat for the evacuation from his observation post in South Carolina. "We could hear the rumbling of wheels as all night long they toiled on," he wrote. "It was too dark to see them, but we knew that they were going." Carman reported his observations, but he was told to sit tight; other Union troops would block the Confederate retreat.[284] Rank-and-file Union soldiers like Theodore Upson were also well aware that the Confederates were absconding. "I think our officers knew they were going and did not try to stop them," he confided to his diary, "for we could hear them all night moving about." While Upson and his comrades were disappointed by the Confederate escape, he concluded, "I am aufuly [*sic*] glad we did not have to charge their works for we would have lost a good many lives, thats sure."[285]

The blue-coated troops stayed put because Sherman had explicitly ordered them to do so. The commanding general had traveled to Hilton Head to meet with his counterpart there, General John G. Foster, to formulate plans to work together to block Hardee's escape route. Sherman left orders for no action to be taken until he returned to his headquarters outside Savannah, so the obvious signs of the Confederate retreat were ignored. Before Sherman's departure, General Henry W. Slocum, one of Sherman's two wing commanders, urged quick action to close off the Union Causeway, the very route Hardee was now using to evade capture. "Damn it! Let us take this plank road and shut these fellows in," Slocum exclaimed.[286] General Carman, too, argued in favor of blocking the road immediately rather than waiting for Foster's troops to move in from the north, but Sherman refused. Disappointed, Carman explained, "My rank did not permit me to press the matter [with Sherman], though I thought a great opportunity was being lost."[287] Sherman wrote in his memoirs that his reluctance to attack resulted from a fear of his troops becoming trapped in the flooded Carolina rice fields behind enemy lines. The general explained that he wished to avoid a fiasco like the October 1861 Battle of Ball's Bluff, Virginia, an embarrassing defeat in which Union forces had been caught on the enemy's side of a river.[288]

As Hardee's troops made their getaway, Savannah descended into chaos and lawlessness. First Sergeant W.H. Andrews of the First Georgia Regulars described a night too terrifying to forget. "Doors were being knocked down, guns were firing in every direction, the bullets flying over and around us," he wrote. "Women and children [were] screaming and rushing in every direction."[289] Who was to blame for the madness? "It was the white scum of the city that came out of their dens like nocturnal beasts to the work of the pillage," remembered George Blount, a Confederate soldier who also witnessed the mayhem. Three companies of Georgia reservists, Companies A, B and K of the Sixth Georgia Regiment, were ordered to stay behind until the last minute and keep order in the city, but this proved to be an impossible task. Blount described what he witnessed on that unforgettable night:

> [We] *were ordered into line and marched double quick to Market Square to protect the stores from the mob which was looting them.... When near Broughton and Whitaker the boys heard the crash of doors before the rush of the robbers. Men, women and children would force open a door like hungry dogs after a bone, each for himself, indifferent to the property rights of others, they would grab, smash, pull, tear, anything, everything, shoes, meat, clothes, soap, hats, whatever came to hand. First they would take, then run to hide their spoils in some place, only to return and swell*

*the crowd at some other point. If you want to know what brutes human
beings can become, wait and watch them in such a time as this was.*

The commanding officer divided the troops into squads and ordered them
to "run up one street, down another clearing store after store of the toughs
and the roughs," remembered Blount, "but it was all in vain, for as soon
as one building would be cleared, they would hear the crash of doors on
another block. It was the same work over and over."[290]

Some of the trouble may actually have been caused by Confederate
soldiers—specifically members of General Joe Wheeler's cavalry. Sergeant
Michael Turrentine of North Carolina wrote to his sister about North
Carolina artillery troops being sent into town to suppress a riot during the
evacuation and shooting several of Wheeler's men in the process. Turrentine
wrote derisively of Wheeler's troopers, "They are the meanest set of men
that ever lived [and] have stolen and destroyed more than the enemy. They
have been guilty of acts that a decent Yankee would be ashamed to commit."
Turrentine added that a number of intoxicated Confederate stragglers were
captured by the advancing Federals.[291]

After the last of the Confederate troops crossed over the pontoon bridge
onto Hutchinson Island, Captain Robert Mackay Stiles, a Confederate
army engineer, cut away the pontoon bridge from the Savannah shore at
5:40 a.m. on December 21, followed by the shorter spans over the middle
and back channels. Stiles and his fellow engineers also drilled holes in the
barges so they would slowly sink, then set them on fire, to make sure Union
troops could not use the vessels to pursue the retreating Confederates.[292]
At the last minute, someone remembered that another company of troops
from the Sixth Georgia Regiment, commanded by Captain Benjamin
Millikin, had been forgotten and was still guarding the Confederate powder
magazine west of the city. Was there time to get word to these abandoned
soldiers and make it possible for them to escape? A few officers raced into
the Exchange building and up the steps to the steeple. Their hearts sank as
they saw Union troops nearing the armory; it was too late. As the Federals
closed in, one of the forsaken Confederates, James Horne, reportedly shot
the first Federal soldier to arrive on the scene. The entire company of
Confederate reserves was captured.[293]

Blount and his comrades left the city aboard the steamer *Swan*, since the
pontoon bridge had already been destroyed.[294] Union soldiers appeared on
West Broad Street as the despondent Confederates pulled away from the
wharf. Blount described the spectacle that accompanied their departure:

A grand, but fearful sight met the eye. Fire, fire, everywhere on the river front.

The rice flats which had formed the pontoon bridge had been set on fire after the army had crossed the river. Some were entirely consumed, others had drifted and lodged against the bank on Hutchinson Island, some were still linked together and were burning fiercely. Others were floating down the river like huge torches.

…The cheeks of the men were warmed by the heat from burning vessels which they passed. Their eyes were weary with looking at the flames, which the river, like a huge mirror, reflected from beneath. The men were subdued in spirit, quiet in voice, and sad at heart.[295]

Throughout the course of this eventful and confusing evening, individual Union commanders summoned the courage to creep over the walls of the just-abandoned Confederate fortifications and see for themselves whether the enemy troops really had departed. Colonel Henry Barnum of New York led one such reconnaissance in person as early as midnight. "Not hearing the voices of the enemy, and not seeing their forms passing before their camp-fires, he suspected that they had evacuated their lines," wrote George Ward Nichols, a member of General Sherman's staff, recounting Barnum's bravery. "Although their camp-fires still burned brightly, no Rebels were to be seen."[296] Around 3:00 a.m., the Confederate guns fell silent, and Union troops began moving en masse into the abandoned Confederate works.[297]

Elsewhere in the Union lines, captains John Henry Otto and Rudolph Weisbrod of Wisconsin conducted their own reconnaissance of the Confederate positions. Otto recounted after the war:

We crept on hands and knees until we were close up to the works. Still all was quiet as in a grave.…I put my Cap aside, put a foot on a projecting log, drew myself up and looked over the top log. Small heaps of dimly glimmering coals were here and there but no human being could be seen.…I whispered to the Sergeant to give me a lift so as to get over without noise. The first thing I did was to feel for the vent of the cannons. They were spicked [spiked, i.e., plugged]. That was proof enough.…The birds had flown.[298]

Wesley De Haven, a soldier in another Wisconsin regiment, was simultaneously more succinct and dismissive of his vanished foe. "The rebels kept up a bold front till 2 o'clock last night," he wrote, "when they ignominiously skedaddled like [the] thieves and scoundrels they are—spiking their guns and leaving the marks of a hurried departure."[299]

Savannah's city council members passed a long and anxious evening in the council chambers at the Exchange building, worrying that Sherman's troops would burn, steal, murder and rape their way into the city. The aldermen decided that their best course of action was to set out in small groups before daylight toward the Union lines, surrender the city to a responsible officer, and beg for protection. Aldermen J.F. O'Byrne and Robert Lachlison were the first to encounter Union troops, on the Augusta Road. A junior officer conducted them to Colonel Barnum, who took them to General Geary at 4:30 a.m. At first, Geary doubted the men's identities, but he listened to them carefully and changed his mind. Geary accepted the surrender of the city and agreed to protect the lives and property of the citizens. A short time later, Lachlison, O'Byrne and their Union escort caught up with Mayor Arnold at the Central of Georgia Railway bridge on the western edge of the city, near the present-day Savannah Visitors Information Center.

Mayor Arnold led Geary and his soldiers up West Broad Street toward the river and east on Bay Street to the Exchange building, which served as the headquarters of municipal government and stood on the spot occupied today by Savannah City Hall. Barnum's exuberant troops cheered with every step. Two-and-a-half-year-old Caroline Couper Stiles peered through the open slat of a shutter in her home and was shocked by what she saw: "From the east there comes pouring a sea of blue-coated soldiers, shouting, leaping, and brandishing their muskets." At 6:15 a.m., the men formed up in ranks in front of the Exchange as the Stars and Stripes and various regimental and division flags were raised above its steeple and also atop the former U.S. Customs House across Bay Street. The troops fell silent as Barnum and Geary addressed them, with Mayor Arnold and the council members standing behind the commanders on the balcony.[300] Afterward, Barnum formed the troops into squads and sent them out to restore order in the city—apparently not a moment too soon. "Within a few hours this city," Geary reported, "in which I had found a lawless mob of low whites and negroes pillaging and setting fire to property, was reduced to order; many millions of dollars' worth of cotton, ordnance, and commissary stores, &c., which would otherwise have been destroyed, were saved." Major George W. Nichols of Sherman's staff echoed Geary's claims, asserting: "It was fortunate that our troops followed so quickly after the evacuation of the city by the enemy, for a mob had gathered in the streets, and were breaking into the stores and houses. They were with difficulty dispersed by the bayonets of our soldiers, and then, once more, order and confidence prevailed throughout the conquered city."[301]

There were still some Confederate forces in Savannah—sailors aboard the powerful ironclad warship CSS *Savannah*. Confederate naval commanders had ordered the *Savannah*'s captain, Commander Thomas W. Brent, to get the ironclad out of harm's way by steaming through Ossabaw Sound and to bring the ship into Charleston, Wilmington, Georgetown or another Confederate-held port. Referring to the *Savannah* and the other, less powerful ships in the Confederate squadron, Captain Sydney Smith Lee instructed Brent:

> *Under any circumstances, it is better for the vessels, for the Navy, for our cause and country, that these vessels should fall in the conflict of battle, taking all the risks of defeat and triumph, than that they should be tamely surrendered to the enemy or destroyed by their own officers. If fall they must, let them show neither the weakness of submission nor of self-destruction, but inflict a blow that will relieve defeat from discredit.* [302]

By the time the American flag waved over the Exchange, all the other vessels of the Confederate navy's Savannah Squadron were captured, scuttled or in flames. The *Savannah* alone remained, its Rebel flag fluttering defiantly in the smoke that hung over the river. Earlier, Captain Brent had made an effort to follow Lee's orders by removing obstructions placed in the river by Confederate engineers, but the devices were planted too firmly in the mud and sand to be removed, even with the assistance of a steam-powered vessel. At least one crew member, Robert Watson, was glad the escape attempt had failed, confiding in his diary, "I fear it will be a dangerous undertaking for the river is full of torpedoes and if we should escape them we would have the whole Yankee fleet to contend with." Since resigning himself to remain in the city, Brent had stationed the *Savannah* near a ferry dock on the South Carolina side of the Savannah River, providing protection for the evacuation of valuable supplies. [303] Before its career as a Confederate warship came to a fiery conclusion, the *Savannah* would fire the only shells lobbed into the city itself—by either side—during the siege and evacuation.

Shortly after 7:00 a.m., just before sunrise, two regiments of Union soldiers from Pennsylvania and Ohio swarmed into Fort Jackson on the Savannah River east of the city, raising the American flag over its brick ramparts. Taking aim at the former Confederate installation, the *Savannah*'s navy gunners fired several shells at the fort. No record survives to indicate whether their gunnery resulted in any damage, nor are there reports of any Union troops being injured. [304] A little more than three hours later, Union field artillery began firing on the *Savannah* from a location near the gasworks, in the vicinity of Trustees Garden. The Federal cannoneers were accurate, but the Rebel sailors were incredibly lucky. "The Yankees made excellent shots," wrote Watson. "Nearly every one struck our sides or smoke stack. One shell went down the smoke stack and rested on the grating but did not explode." The Southerners quickly returned fire, but the Union position was so high on the bluff that the *Savannah*'s crew could not angle their own guns steeply enough to reach them. "We were not slow in returning the compliment," said Watson, adding ruefully, "but with what effect I cannot say." The Union firing ceased shortly before noon, but resumed in late afternoon and continued into the evening.[305] At least one of the *Savannah*'s shells caused damage to a "friendly" structure, exploding in front of a house at the northwest corner of Lincoln and Broughton Streets and tearing a long strip of weatherboarding off the exterior of the house. The *Savannah Morning News* asserted seven years later, "This was the only house in Savannah that was struck by shot or shell during the siege." A correspondent for the *Chicago Tribune*, however, claimed that "many of the shots fired by the ram went into the city, entering dwellings and storehouses, and unsettling chimneys, to the infinite disgust of the citizens." The truth may never be known.[306]

The *Savannah* would wreak no more havoc on any target, Union or Confederate. That evening, seeing no way to save his ship from capture, Commander Brent ordered his crew to disembark. Brent informed his superiors, "I considered it my duty to destroy my ship to prevent her from falling into the hands of the enemy, and to save the officers and crew." Brent and his executive officer, Lieutenant William E. Hudgins, were among the last to leave. As they departed, the commanders set the ship ablaze. The *Savannah*'s sailors turned their backs on the ship and began marching, joining the long, gray line moving into South Carolina. "Nothing was saved except what was carried about the person," Brent reported, "and no transportation could be obtained from the army except a wagon to carry the sick, who could not march."[307]

It took just less than four hours for the flames to reach the seven and a half tons of powder and hundreds of shells left aboard the burning ship. John Chipman Gray, a military lawyer on General John G. Foster's staff, witnessed the explosion from the steamboat *Canonicus* in Lazaretto Creek east of Savannah. "I saw the red light," he wrote, "suddenly shoot up into a tall fiery column with a ball of thick black smoke at its summit, and soon afterwards we heard the explosion which shook the windows even at Hilton Head." The *Savannah*'s crew had already marched between six and eight miles, but they were still able to hear, see and feel the death of their ship. Watson wrote, "It was terrific, it lit the heavens for miles, we could see to pick up a pin where we were and the noise was awful."[308]

Another CSS *Savannah* sailor, Iverson "Dutt" Graves, was heartbroken by the loss of his ship and all it represented but found a remedy close at hand:

> *You have no idea what a sad blow it was to me. Thinks I, there goes my pleasant quarters, my good clothes, my good warm overcoat, and I am forever cut off from Savannah and the hope of ever making myself agreeable to the Savannah girls; my heart sank within me, my limbs ached, my load was terribly heavy, and my eyelids had a mutual attraction for each other. But I thought of my canteen which I had been provident enough to fill with whiskey, and taking a good swig, I felt the generous fluid to course through every vein and fill me with fresh strength and spirit.*[309]

As the Southern sailors joined their army comrades in the long march into South Carolina, General Sherman was aboard a boat attempting to return to Savannah following his strategy session with General Foster

The crew of the ironclad CSS *Savannah* blew up their own ship, then joined the long line of Confederate troops evacuating into South Carolina. *Hargrett Rare Book & Manuscript Library, University of Georgia.*

and Admiral Dahlgren at Hilton Head. Another boat approached with news that the Confederates had taken flight and Union forces were now in possession of the city. "I was disappointed that Hardee had escaped with his army," Sherman wrote in his memoirs, "but on the whole we had reason to be content with the substantial fruits of victory." Writing to Major General Henry W. Halleck a few days after the capture of Savannah, Sherman declared, "I felt somewhat disappointed at Hardee's escape from me, but really am not to blame. I moved as quick as possible… but intervening obstacles were such that before I could get my troops on the road Hardee had slipped out." In truth, given the many alarms raised by his field commanders before and during Hardee's escape, it is clear Sherman could have acted much more decisively had he wished to do so. Perhaps Sherman never really intended to catch Hardee at all; it was easier to starve the Confederates out or simply turn a blind eye while they escaped. This was the assessment of John Chipman Gray, who wrote, "I think it likely he would have allowed him to march out with his army for the sake of getting immediate possession of the city, so perhaps it is all for the best."[310]

Other observers, both Union and Confederate, were much less kind in their characterizations of Sherman's inaction. A frustrated General Ezra Carman bemoaned, "had he indicated that energy which was his characteristic…the probabilities are that he would have captured Hardee and the entire Confederate garrison of Savannah." Colonel Charles C. Jones Jr., who commanded Confederate light artillery during the siege, inveighed, "all the balderdash which has been written and spoken about this vaunted 'march to the sea' can never, in the clear light of history, cover up or excuse the lack of dash and the want of military skill betrayed by General Sherman…in permitting the Confederate garrison to retire unmolested."[311]

And what about Hardee? How did the Confederate commander view his own deeds of December 20–21, 1864? One might expect the "ignominious" retreat to be a source of embarrassment to this career military professional. But looking back on the successful removal of ten thousand mostly untested soldiers right under the noses of six times as many well-supplied Union troops, Hardee wrote after the war, "Tho' compelled to evacuate the city, there is no part of my military life to which I look back with so much satisfaction."[312] Sergeant Turrentine of North Carolina echoed his commander's sentiment, writing:

To all who speak ill of Hardee say that it is to his skill and indomitable energy that the South owes the rescue of ten thousand of his troops. If we had remained there two days longer we would have been captured. The construction of the pontoon bridge in the number of days which it occupied and out of such material was truly astonishing and reflects credit upon the head which directed it.[313]

AFTER THE FALL

Savannah Rejoins the Union

If there is one sink lower than any other in the abyss of degradation the people of Savannah have reached it.
—Augusta Daily Constitutionalist, *March 1, 1865*

Considering the fiery pro-Confederate rhetoric coming from Savannah's pulpits, politicians and newspapers over more than three years of war, one might expect an angry, defiant citizenry to greet General Sherman on his entry into Savannah. One would be sorely disappointed, however, for within one week of the surrender of the city on December 21, 1864, Savannah's leading citizens indicated their desire to abandon the Confederacy and return to the Federal fold.

When he arrived in the city, Sherman wrote, "The mayor, Dr. Arnold, was completely 'subjugated.'"[314] Consequently, the general issued written orders for the mayor and city council to remain in office and work together with the occupying army to maintain order, clean and light the streets and make sure firefighters stayed on the job.[315] Whether Mayor Arnold had lost his Confederate patriotism or simply considered cooperation to be the only way to revive the city—or both—is an unanswered question.

Regardless of his motives, it seems the mayor had the pulse of his people, for on December 27, 1864—six days after the capture of the city—the following petition arrived on his desk:

General William T. Sherman's Union troops enter Savannah and march down Bay Street on December 21, 1864. *Hargrett Rare Book & Manuscript Library, University of Georgia.*

We, the citizens of Savannah, believing that the interests of the city demands that immediate action be taken to get the voice of the people upon matters relating to her present and future welfare, respectfully request that a meeting of the citizens be called on Wednesday, 28th inst., at 12 o'clock, in the Exchange Long Rooms, to give them that opportunity to express themselves in reference to the city's welfare.[316]

Dozens of leading citizens, including Gazaway Bugg Lamar, attached their signatures.

Accordingly, the mayor called a public meeting at the Masonic Hall at noon the next day, December 28.[317] According to one estimate, at least seven hundred people attended.[318] In order that people would feel able to speak freely, no Union soldiers or officers were permitted inside, and sentinels were placed at the door to keep the soldiers out.[319] Voting by vocal acclamation, the assembled citizens passed the following resolutions:[320]

WHEREAS, By the fortunes of war and the surrender of the city by the civil authorities, the city of Savannah passes once more under the authority of the United States; and whereas, we believe that the interests of the city will be best subserved [sic] *and promoted by a full and free expression of our views in relation to our present condition; we, therefore, the People of Savannah in full meeting assembled do hereby resolve:*

That we accept the position, and in the language of the President of the United States, seek to have "peace by laying down our arms and submitting to the National authority under the Constitution, leaving all questions which remain to be adjusted by the peaceful means of legislation, conference, and votes."

Resolved, That laying aside all differences, and burying by-gones [sic] *in the grave of the past, we will use our best endeavors once more to bring back the prosperity and commerce we once enjoyed.*

Resolved, That we do not put ourselves in the position of a conquered city, asking terms of a conqueror, but we claim the immunities and privileges contained in the Proclamation and Message of the President of the United States and in all the legislation of Congress in reference to a people situated as we are, and while we owe on our part a strict obedience to the laws of the United States, we ask the protection over our persons, lives and property recognized by these laws.

Resolved, That we respectfully request His Excellency the Governor, to call a Convention of the people of Georgia, by any Constitutional means in his power, to give them an opportunity of voting upon the question whether they wish the war between the two sections of the country to continue.[321]

Savannah was back in the Union—not just as a captured, surrendered or subjugated city, but as a willing participant in the political life of the United States. And this vote took place in the very building where, four years, three months and eleven days earlier, the late Francis S. Bartow declared, "I am a Union man in every fibre [sic] of my heart."[322] This was certainly not the outcome Bartow had in mind when he made his declaration.

Not surprisingly, the blowback from Savannah's Confederate sister cities and diehard Confederate sympathizers was swift and severe. "Savannah has gone down on her knees and humbly begged pardon of Father Abraham, gratefully acknowledging Sherman's clemency in burning and laying waste their State!" snarled Emma Le Conte.[323] "These miserable Sycophants," hissed the *Augusta Daily Constitutionalist.* "If there is one sink lower than any other in the abyss of degradation the people of Savannah have reached it."[324] The *Richmond Times-Dispatch* made a personal attack on Mayor Arnold, comparing him to the infamous Revolutionary War traitor of the same surname, and concluded, "This meeting, then, proves nothing, except what all knew before; that there are traitorous and weak kneed people in Savannah, as there are here, and in every other Confederate city....Sherman has made the Mayor of Savannah slander the people of the State. That is all."[325]

Northern observers were not so convinced of the sincerity of Savannah's supplication. A correspondent for the *New York Times* who was in the city at the time of the public meeting wrote, "I would not be understood to say that the spirit of secession is wholly dead in Savannah, but only that a strong Union sentiment is gradually winning its way among the citizens."[326] A committee of Bostonians who visited Savannah reported, "There have always been in Savannah a *few really* and *thoroughly* loyal Union men....But the far larger class, which we think includes nearly all the male population of the city, are those who are convinced of the hopelessness of the rebel cause."[327]

The only noteworthy exceptions to this generalization, wrote the Bostonians, were Savannah's female citizens. "The women," wrote the Northerners, "are still ardent advocates of the rebel cause....Many have lost husbands, sons, and brothers in the struggle, and are not yet willing to admit that all the sacrifices, hardships, and sufferings of the past four years, together with the blood which has been shed, shall all be in vain."[328]

Political convictions notwithstanding, those very women found a way to profit from the occupation of their city by selling homemade baked goods. Elizabeth Georgia Basinger's brother William was still in the field commanding the Savannah Volunteer Guards, but she was more than willing to sell sweets to his enemies, exclaiming, "Come, let us up and be doing! These Yankees all want something sweet and we want some greenbacks."[329] The basements of many of Savannah's finest mansions were converted into bake shops, as reported by artist W.T. Crane in *Frank Leslie's Illustrated Newspaper*:

> *It represents a scene of daily occurrences in Savannah. In front of some of the finest residences in the city, whose upper storeys* [sic] *are closed entirely, you will find in the basements elegantly dressed ladies and servants disposing of cakes and other delicacies to our brave boys, who invariably give postal currency and greenbacks for these luxuries, prepared under the superintendence of the fair daughters of chivalry. I could not help saying as I gazed on this curious change in the whirligig of time, "How are the mighty fallen!"*[330]

Savannahians were willing to rejoin the Union in order to escape the suffering caused by four years of war. *Author's collection.*

In order to provide context for his Northern readers, Crane's editor added, "It is tantamount to our Astors, Belmonts, Haights, Stevenses, Stewarts and Lorillards turning cake-vendors here to gain a little Confederate scrip." But this humble business offered meaningful reward for the defeated women. One Savannah lady told General Sherman she was able to realize a $56 profit—more than $800 in 2016 currency values—by selling pies and cakes baked with flour and sugar she received from the occupiers.[331]

The women were not the only former Confederates ready to turn a profit from the new order in Savannah. Soon after Sherman established authority, a group of merchants prepared to journey to New York on the next northbound steamer, ready to "win back the commerce of which the rebellion robbed their fair city, and to restore it to more than its former prosperity," according to the *New York Times* correspondent.[332]

Savannah didn't want just to be back in the Union—it wanted to be back in business.

WHO SAYS SHERMAN DIDN'T BURN SAVANNAH?

The Great Fire of January 1865

Never while I live shall I cease to remember this night of horrors.
—*William Brown Hodgson*

O ne of the questions most frequently posed by visitors to tour guides in Savannah is "Why didn't General Sherman burn Savannah?" The answer to that question, of course, is that Sherman had no reason to burn the city; the Confederate army evacuated Savannah in the dead of night, leaving Sherman and his tired soldiers a relatively safe, comfortable place to rest after their long March to the Sea. But the answer belies a hidden truth: a large portion of Savannah did burn under Sherman's watch. The only question is, who burned it?

It happened on the evening of Friday, January 27, 1865, five weeks after Sherman's arrival in the city and mere days before his departure for the second act of his destructive campaign—the march through the Carolinas. The blaze began in a stable behind the home of a Mrs. Morrell and soon spread throughout the entire northwestern portion of the city, driven by a strong northerly wind. In the beginning, "dense volumes of smoke were discovered issuing from the large double tenement four-story brick building on the north side of Broughton-street," according to the *Savannah Daily Loyal Republican*.[333] The alarm bell in the Exchange building rang, summoning the city's firefighters into action. Apparently, however, no one took the alarm very seriously at first. "At ten o'clock there was a cry of fire, but that cry was so frequent we paid no attention to it," wrote one Savannah resident.[334] A visitor who wandered the streets during the early moments of the fire noted, "The fire engines were deserted, and the fire was having its own way, licking up the buildings, one after another, remorselessly."[335] *Harper's Weekly* rounded out the chorus of damning criticism, alleging, "Owing to the inactivity of the Fire Department the flames spread rapidly."[336]

Everything changed when, sometime between 11:00 p.m. and midnight, the flames reached the former Confederate naval arsenal, known as Granite Hall, at the corner of West Broad and Zubly Streets. Hundreds of artillery shells and cannonballs—up to one thousand, by some estimates—were stored there, and within minutes, they began rocketing through the air, exploding above the city and sending shrapnel flying in all directions. A young Confederate nurse named Janet Howard wrote in her diary:

> *At a quarter to twelve Nelly and I were awakened by the explosion of a shell.…We sprang from our beds and, looking out of the window, found the fire raging in West Broad Street.…The bursting of the shells now became terrific, pieces of them falling all around our house, and we could hear them striking the houses around us.*
>
> *The heavens were as light as day, while the bursting shells sent up jets of smoke and flame high above the burning houses. The sight itself was grand beyond description. Not a sound could be heard in the street below. The few awestricken people, who were seeking safety in flight, crept silently along as close to the walls as possible, and then sped like lightning across the street.*[337]

"People rushed from their houses, half-dressed," reported the *Savannah Daily Herald*, a Union publication that had taken over the press of the former *Savannah Morning News*. Guests at the Pulaski House hotel ran down the stairs in breathless panic, thinking the city was under surprise attack by the Confederate army. Among them was famed Northern war correspondent Charles Coffin. "I was awakened by a sudden explosion, which jarred the house," he recalled. "There was another explosion, then a volley of shells, and large fragments came whirring through the air, striking the walls, or falling with a heavy plunge into the street." Coffin ran out of the building and was awestruck by the spectacle he beheld. "It was a gorgeous sight," he remembered, "the flames leaping high in air, thrown up in columns by the thirteen-inch shells, filling the air with burning timbers, cinders, and myriads of sparks."[338]

Union soldiers hauled wagons full of unexploded shells to the river and tossed them into the water to prevent further explosions. *City of Savannah Research Library and Municipal Archives.*

The Union troops who occupied the captured city rushed into the flickering semidarkness, risking their lives in the midst of a bombardment nearly as dangerous as any ever unleashed on them by Confederate artillery. Using an old wooden wagon they pulled by hand, a brave group of soldiers ferried unexploded shells away from the encroaching flames.[339] Yet the blaze continued unabated. "Between twelve and one the scene was sadly, savagely grand," observed the *Daily Herald*. "The flames from the burning piles of buildings had spread in one lurid sheet over the city with a black cloud of smoke like a funeral pile hovering over them. Every moment hissing, shrieking shells would mount in the air, dashing their hurtling fragments around."[340]

A shell crashed into the bedroom where Laura Winkler Palmer was sleeping. It was a sickening turn of events for a young mother left alone with her children after the evacuation of her Confederate soldier husband a few weeks earlier. Terrified, Palmer and the youngsters fled outside and hid under a porch. A Union soldier came to the rescue, coaxing the family back inside the house and starting a fire in the fireplace to keep them warm.[341]

Meanwhile, a human drama was unfolding on the streets beneath the incendiary spectacle. Women and children rushed about in terror, alternately darting into their homes or blindly fleeing the screaming shells. Families were separated in the midst of the confusion. "Women and children were huddled in groups under shelter of walls and houses, trembling both with cold and fear," the *Herald* continued ominously. "The scene it presented was heart-rending in the extreme.…We have seen towns sacked, we have witnessed many a battle field, but so fearfully grand and appalling a sight we have scarcely ever witnessed."

A correspondent for the *New York Times* sprang into action to help wounded Confederate prisoners of war who were trapped in a hospital that was threatened by the flames. "I would find them crouched down on the walk, under the fence and walls, to escape the flying shells, having staggered out of the hospital in their fright, some crawling, who had suffered amputation," he wrote. Shocked that no Savannahians were coming to the aid of the endangered Rebel soldiers, the Northern journalist gathered a small group of men and went to work. "I passed the entire night, till five o'clock in the morning," he claimed, "dragging those poor fellows through the streets and getting them into beds."[342]

The most heart-stopping moments of the long night transpired outside the aforementioned four-story tenement house on the north side of Broughton Street, when flames cut off the only means of escape for the people trapped inside. The *Savannah Loyal Republican* described the drama that unfolded:

As soon as it became known that there were several persons still in the building, including women and children, unable to escape, a thrill of fearful horror ran through the vast crowd and the greatest excitement prevailed. Presently the windows in the second and third stories were opened, and there at the casemates could be dimly discerned the forms of three or four women—one a terrified mother clasping her innocent infant in her arms. The multitude cheer and shout, rending the air with their cries of warning, "Jump for your lives, we'll save you;" "for God's sake jump, woman;" "jump on to the mattress, no danger;" "jump, we'll catch you," &c., while an expression of the deepest solicitude and horror was depicted upon the upturned sea of anxious faces. Brave men, with stout hearts, stood ready with mattresses to rescue the inmates, if they could only be prevailed upon to take the fearful leap for life. Higher and more dense arose the clouds of smoke each moment, and soon the forked flames hissed savagely, threatening the total destruction of the building. No time was to be lost. Either the dizzy leap must be made or all would perish. Through the nebulous film that partly obscured the form of the panic-stricken women who stood shuddering with dismay, we caught the glimpse of a woman preparing to jump from the third story. More hearty cheers rolled up from the trembling crowd; one woman seeing no hope of escape from the horrible fate that was momentarily threatening her, jumped and was caught on a large mattress by the soldiers, sustaining no injury beyond a slight shock and considerable fright. From the second-story window, a fond mother threw her babe upon the mattress and jumped out immediately after it. Both were rescued without injury save the slight concussion, by the noble veterans.

The first occupant who plunged from the building was a colored woman, who was caught in the arms of the soldiers. As soon as it was ascertained that all were saved, a wild shout of joy went up, and each soldier appeared anxious to test the full capacity of his lungs.[343]

As the fire spread and grew in size, it became a threat to the vessels tied up in the harbor. A shell fragment struck the steamer *Daniel Webster*, but remarkably, the ship was not damaged. The madness reached its apex when

GREAT FIRE AT SAVANNAH, GA., JAN. 27TH—RESERVOIR BURST BY THE SHELLS.—FROM A SKETCH BY OUR SPECIAL ARTIST, W. T. CRANE.

A flying shell from the burning Confederate armory pierced the water tower in Franklin Square, sending a shimmering torrent of water cascading down. *City of Savannah Research Library and Municipal Archives.*

108

a flying shell pierced the water tower that stood in the center of Franklin Square, sending a torrent of water cascading to the ground, "rivaling in beauty any fountain, and looking in the fiery glare like a shower of molten silver," the *Daily Herald* breathlessly declared.[344]

The explosions gradually subsided by 2:00 a.m., by which time the ammunition had been exhausted, though firefighting efforts continued throughout the night. When the sun rose the next morning, it illuminated an awful scene. "The streets and walks were covered with fragments of broken shells," the *Daily Herald* announced, describing "a heap of ruins" strewn with "smoking piles." Even the trees were "shattered and torn."

More than one hundred buildings were destroyed in the little-known Savannah fire of January 27–28, 1865. *Library of Congress.*

The fire left many Savannahians homeless during the coldest time of the year, adding to the woes of the already suffering citizens. *Library of Congress.*

Charles Coffin called the burned area "a wilderness of chimneys," where "the streets were strewn with furniture." More than one hundred buildings were destroyed, and many more damaged, during the coldest time of the year. Newly homeless women and children could be seen weeping over the ruins of their homes, and burned bodies were lying here and there on the streets. The *Daily Herald* reporter stumbled across a corpse at the corner of Broughton and West Broad and recoiled in horror. "It presented a most ghastly spectacle," he wrote. "All the flesh and hair and some of the limbs were burned into cinders, while the head and trunk remained, presenting the appearance of a much decayed mummy."[345] After surviving the Confederate evacuation and Sherman's arrival unscathed, Savannahians could barely comprehend the level of destruction that had so suddenly befallen their city. "Never while I live," wrote William Brown Hodgson of the inferno, "shall I cease to remember this night of horrors."[346]

No one will ever know for certain how the conflagration began. When smaller fires were discovered in several buildings in other parts of town, some people concluded that all of the blazes were intentionally started by someone—but whom? Not surprisingly, many Savannahians blamed Sherman's soldiers—particularly the troops of his Twentieth Corps, who feared they would be left behind to garrison Savannah and would consequently miss out on the pleasures of his coming march through the Carolinas.[347] Others blamed Confederate saboteurs. The blaze could just as easily have been an accident, like the many other great fires that devoured large portions of Savannah over the years.

Regardless of who was to blame, the fact remains that Savannah did burn after Sherman arrived; furthermore, it would not be terribly inaccurate to say the city came under artillery attack as well.

SILENCE AND THE SENTINEL

Savannah's Confederate Memory

Come from the four winds, O Breath, and Breathe upon these slain,
that they may live.
—Ezekiel 37:9 (quoted on a panel of Savannah's Confederate Monument)

Perched atop a sandstone pedestal, a solitary bronze Confederate soldier keeps silent watch fifty feet above the sweeping green expanse of Savannah's Forsyth Park. Just over half a mile to the southwest, in Laurel Grove Cemetery, stands a robed female figure carved from Italian marble. With her right finger raised to her lips to command silence, she gazes eternally on a field of more than seven hundred granite headstones, each marking the final resting place of a Confederate soldier. Though they survey disparate domains and are crafted in divergent styles from very different materials, these two sculptures are chapters of the same story: she once stood inside the shaft of the monument in Forsyth Park, and both statues were born of an early postwar effort to properly honor the Southern soldiers buried in Laurel Grove.

The tale of both statues begins in the winter of 1867, less than two years after the last Confederate army surrendered and almost a decade before either figure was created and set into place. Georgia was still an occupied state, and Savannah's streets were patrolled by U.S. Army troops. It was inappropriate for Southern men to create any overt symbols of loyalty to the defeated Confederate cause, but it was perfectly acceptable for Southern women to mourn the region's fallen soldiers, since grief and mourning—considered appropriate sentiments in the realm of women at the time—wore neither blue nor gray. Throughout the region, ladies' memorial associations were formed to tend to the graves of thousands of Confederate troops. On February 15, 1867, the *Savannah Daily News and Herald* published a letter from an anonymous local woman, who wrote,

> *We hear of Memorial Associations being formed in every city and town where lay any number of Confederate dead. Will Savannah be the exception when we have in our cemetery upwards of five hundred uncared for graves of Confederate soldiers [?] Shall the last resting place of the brave men who gave their lives in defence of our cause continue to be neglected until their humble graves are overgrown and obliterated? We trust not, and feel confident that no Southern woman will refuse to give her mite to aid in preserving them. All who feel an interest in the subject, and who are willing to form a Memorial Association, are invited to meet at the Independent Presbyterian Sunday School room on Monday afternoon at half-past four o'clock.* [348]

A large number of women attended the first meeting on February 18. The group formally incorporated itself as the Ladies Memorial Association, and initially, their efforts were focused entirely on the more than five hundred Confederate military graves located in Laurel Grove Cemetery—now referred to as Laurel Grove North, to differentiate this predominantly white burying ground from the African American Laurel Grove South located nearby.

Once again following a trend set by some other Southern cities, the Savannah ladies voted to observe April 26 as Confederate Memorial Day; this was the day that General Joseph Johnston's surrender to General William T. Sherman in North Carolina went into effect in 1865, effectively ending the war. [349]

The first Confederate Memorial Day brought hundreds to Laurel Grove Cemetery. For many, it was likely the first opportunity since the end of the war to grieve openly for the bitter losses suffered over four years of conflict. Soldiers' graves were covered with wreathes, flowers, fabric—even moss torn from the limbs of trees. One mass grave containing the bodies of eleven soldiers killed in the same battle on the same day in April 1865 was festooned with a pencil drawing rendered on satin cloth and a poem by well-known Confederate poet Carrie Belle Sinclair. "We think not a grave was neglected," the *Daily News and Herald* proclaimed, continuing:

The scene yesterday at Laurel Grove was very impressive. All the avenues leading to the graveyard were crowded with carriages and persons on foot, bearing in their hands some token for the departed loved one. In the miscellaneous crowd which thronged the cemetery, here and there might be seen the sad, expressive face of a mother, sister or widow, whose offering was accompanied by tears.[350]

With the first Confederate Memorial Day now in the history books, the Ladies Memorial Association shifted its focus to the permanent care of the graves in Laurel Grove, many of which were crudely marked and dug in haste. The burials dated to the earliest days of the conflict and continued through early 1865 to include wounded prisoners who had died after Sherman captured the city the previous December.[351] In 1868, the ladies decided to enclose a single lot, which is today commonly referred to as Confederate Field, at Laurel Grove.[352] Former Confederate general Jeremy Gilmer, who had been a military engineer, agreed to procure and install iron fencing around the graves. Posts for the enclosure were made of stone from Stone Mountain, Georgia, and the iron railing was crafted at Tredegar Works in Richmond.[353] Starting in mid-1869, Confederate military burials scattered throughout Laurel Grove were disinterred and moved to Confederate Field at the City of Savannah's expense, making the Ladies Memorial Association's tasks more convenient and freeing up space for new civilian burials.[354] Temporary wooden headstones marked the relocated graves until 1873, when the association replaced them with stone tiles.[355] In 1875, the *Savannah Morning News* noted, "In due time neat headboards were erected to mark the last resting place of our heroes. Wherever it was possible the names of the deceased were inscribed on these simple tablets."[356]

The lifeless army in Confederate Field would soon receive reinforcements—the remains of soldiers who perished at the Battle of Gettysburg in July 1863. The U.S. government created Gettysburg National Cemetery immediately following the battle, ensuring honorable burials for fallen Federal troops. But because the battle was a Union victory and the battlefield was located deep within enemy territory, there was no way for Confederate authorities, who were struggling simply to feed, clothe and equip their armies in the field, to adequately inter the remains of their own dead. Consequently, thousands remained buried in shallow graves where they fell in combat. Beginning in 1871, newspapers printed disturbing reports about Northern farmers plowing through Confederate burials. Ladies Memorial Associations from many areas, starting with one in Wake County, North Carolina, began to organize an effort to exhume the Confederate bodies and bring them home for proper burial. Dr. Rufus Weaver, whose late father, Samuel, a teamster, had been paid to exhume Union battlefield dead for reinterment in the National Cemetery, began the grim work of digging up, identifying and shipping out the Southern bodies. In all, Weaver processed 3,320 sets of Confederate remains. Of these, Savannah received at least 101, all from Georgia units.[357]

The first shipment of Confederate Gettysburg remains arrived in Savannah aboard the steamship *America* on August 22, 1871. Within the steamer's hold were three large caskets containing the bones of thirty-two soldiers. A second shipment of sixty-eight skeletons reached the city just over a month later on September 24. In both instances, the large caskets were conveyed from the wharves to the council chamber in the Exchange building—the same room where the bodies of Francis Bartow and later six of his young soldiers lay in state after their deaths in the war's first major battle. An unwitting visitor from that year might be given the impression that the Confederacy was still fighting in 1871, for, as the *Savannah Morning News* noted, as the Gettysburg remains lay in state, "On all sides were stacks of musketry and flags, while a sentinel…in his suit of loved and honored grey, paced with measured tread back and forth as watchman of the dead." After sufficient time had passed for citizens to pay their respects, Confederate veterans carried the caskets from the Exchange to Laurel Grove, where they were laid to rest alongside the hundreds of other Confederate soldiers who died in and around Savannah during the war. Wartime veterans of local military units took part in the procession, though apparently they were not wearing Confederate uniforms. The official end of Reconstruction, and the restoration of full statehood for Georgia, was still a few months away, and these quasi-military processions were possibly the first public gatherings of former Confederates to take place in Savannah since the end of the war. "Never, in the history of our city, has a more quiet, melancholy, and sadly appreciated occasion been before our people," reported the *Morning News*. "The ladies present, numbering several hundred, came forward and strewed flowers upon the graves so that they were literally covered with floral offerings." After the caskets were lowered into the ground, a police honor guard fired a salute.[358]

The successful return of the Gettysburg remains was a signal success, but the proud Southern women of Savannah wished to do more than just care for the remains of their fallen heroes; they longed to create a lasting tribute to the bravery and courage of the Confederate dead. As early as 1868, the Ladies Memorial Association approved a plan to raise funds to build a monument at Confederate Field in Laurel Grove.[359] Fundraising efforts ran the gamut from collections gathered during the annual Confederate Memorial Day observances at the cemetery to lectures, concerts, festivals and fairs. The first major fundraiser, a multiday fair in December 1869, netted more than $4,000. The ladies shrewdly invested the proceeds, more than doubling the total within four years.[360] In April 1870, former Confederate general Robert E. Lee, who was visiting Savannah, agreed to sit for a photo with fellow former commander Joseph E. Johnston, who lived in the city, to help raise funds for the memorial. Association members sold cartes de visite of the two heroes to grow the fund.[361] In 1873, anxious to erect a monument, the ladies voted "to devote *all money* coming to them from whatever source to the Monument fund." They also decided to ask the city for permission to place the monument in the military parade ground south of the fountain in Forsyth Park, thereby formally abandoning their earlier plan to erect the monument in Laurel Grove Cemetery.[362]

While the ladies themselves took care of the fundraising, they named a committee of four men to supervise the actual procurement and erection of the monument and placed the well-connected and capable General Gilmer in charge. In addition to his status as a former Confederate commander, Gilmer was president of the Savannah Gas Light Company and a director of the Central of Georgia Railroad.[363] On April 19, 1873, Gilmer presented to the ladies a design by Canadian sculptor Robert Reid of Montreal. Gilmer left behind no explanation of why he searched so far afield for a designer or how he found Reid, but the Canadian connection is not too surprising given the fact that many prominent ex-Confederates, including former Confederate president Jefferson Davis and his family, went into temporary exile in Canada after the war.[364]

Reid's design was rendered in a short-lived style termed "modern Italian." It featured an ornately carved sandstone shaft, topped with the heroic, seven-foot, ten-inch marble figure of a woman referred to alternately as "Judgement" or "The Resurrection." In her right hand, Judgement held a trumpet, calling for the attention of the universe; in her left was a scroll, on which was to be written, "The deeds of the noble dead are submitted to the High Court of Eternal Right, Truth and Justice. Feeling sure that our cause was just, we await with calm confidence the final decree of the High Tribunal that cannot err!" Another larger-than-life marble female figure, "Silence," stood beneath her sister within a canopied niche inside the sandstone shaft. "Silence" was depicted touching her right forefinger to

Savannah's Confederate Monument, as originally erected in 1875, featured two marble female figures. Savannahians found the design too elaborate to suit their tastes. *Collection of Hugh Golson.*

her upper lip, demanding quiet and respect for the dead heroes. An inverted torch dangled from her left hand, signifying that the time of destruction and desolation brought by the war had passed. The shaft itself was elaborately carved with such details as guns, swords and furled flags as well as urns and garlands standing out in bold relief. This assemblage stood atop a square stone base, with three of its faces carved in relief. The carving on the north panel depicted another female figure, representing the South in mourning. She was framed by weeping willow trees, frequently used in the nineteenth century to signify mourning and grief. The panel on the east side was inscribed, in capital letters, with a verse from the Old Testament: "COME

FROM THE FOUR WINDS, O BREATH, AND BREATHE UPON THESE SLAIN, THAT THEY MAY LIVE." The text refers to the story of the "dry bones" in Ezekiel 37:9. The sculptor was expressing the sentiment that perhaps God could reanimate the Confederate dead in the same way he had turned skeletons into a living army in the prophet's vision. The panel on the opposite side was inscribed simply, "TO THE CONFEDERATE DEAD 1861–1865." The panel on the south face was left blank. The square base itself rested on a six-foot-tall, forty-square-foot earthwork terrace, with stone stairs leading up to the top of the flat-topped hill on side. On a pedestal on each corner stood a life-sized marble statue of a soldier, with the navy, infantry, cavalry and artillery each represented. The entire monument, as proposed, stood fifty feet tall from ground level beneath the earth work base to the top of the crowning statue.[365] The design was favorably received, with one observer labeling it "one of the most elaborate and elegant I have ever seen."[366]

As it was expected that other designs would be submitted, the ladies postponed a vote until their next meeting. However, there is no record of any other designs being submitted or considered.[367] On July 12, 1873, the association awarded the contract to Reid and paid him $13,600 in gold, out of an overall estimated cost of $24,000.[368] Since the total amount in the association's coffers was just $9,964 at the time the contract was awarded, the ladies doubled down on their ongoing fundraising efforts, with more festivals, fairs and performances.[369] The women also decided to hang a framed copy of Reid's design at the gate to Laurel Grove during the activities there on the next Confederate Memorial Day.[370] The *Savannah Morning News* urged its readers to take action, declaring, "The men of Savannah can now step forward and by timely aid, relieve the ladies from further toil and anxiety."[371]

With a design chosen and fundraising in full swing, the biggest question remaining was where to place the monument. After abandoning their earlier plan to erect the memorial in Confederate Field at Laurel Grove, the Ladies Memorial Association now revisited its decision to build in Forsyth Park instead. In April 1873, the association invited Reid to visit Savannah in person to select the perfect spot for his creation. The sculptor accepted the invitation and spent several days in the city canvassing squares and parks. In the end, Reid concurred with the plan to erect the monument in Forsyth Park, and in April 1874, the association voted to move forward with that location.[372]

The decision ignited a firestorm of criticism, mostly from Confederate veterans who thought the park, which was then at the southern edge of the city, was too far out of town. "In my humble opinion," wrote one unnamed veteran, "the monument should be located in the most conspicuous place in the city, where it would daily greet the eyes of our people, and not in an unimproved field, nearly at the extremity of the city, where it will only be seen on special occasions....It really seems to me that placing such a structure...in a vacant field, devoid of all attractions, is almost equivalent to burying it from public view." The former soldier voiced concern that vandals could harm the isolated monument, and hinted that perhaps it might wind up serving as the backdrop for unsavory political rallies.[373]

In a sweeping defense of their decision printed in the *Savannah Morning News* on May 7, 1874, the members of the association's male monument committee made the case for locating the memorial in Forsyth Park. It was important that the monument be taller than any trees, steeples or surrounding buildings, they argued, and even at fifty feet tall, the memorial would be overshadowed if it were located in any of the major squares. Furthermore, the structures around the squares were so densely packed that it would be impossible for a viewer to see the entire monument unless he stood in the middle of the street. In Forsyth Park, on the other hand, "The ground is open and unobstructed by trees or other objects....Good points of view from every direction can be had." While the squares were dusty, busy places, Forsyth Park was "far removed from the dust of the streets, and therefore free in a measure from soil and stain." Contrasting the park with several of the city's most important squares, the committee argued:

> *Court House square* [Wright Square], *with its busy, active throng and its angry election excitements, was deemed in direct antagonism with the sad and solemn sentiment of the monument, and Chippewa square even more so, with the sights and sounds of the theatre so near—peaceful and quiet surroundings seemed the only suitable ones to carry out and intensify the ideas expressed in the silent stone. In Madison square the trees are more numerous and of denser foliage than in the squares first examined, and the dust equally abundant.*

As far as the fears of vandalism were concerned—well, that could just as easily happen in a square as in a park. And while the park might seem far from town now, Savannah was already growing in that direction, and the city was sure to surround the green space in due time. But perhaps the most poignant argument for locating the monument in Forsyth Park was the fact that the area had served as a parade and drilling ground for many of the same Confederate troops the memorial was designed to honor. "It was on this ground that many of these very men were encamped and drilled in preparation for the bloody work in which their lives were the sacrifice. What spot could be more appropriate on which to commemorate that sacrifice and recall their heroic example?" asked the committee.[374]

The association called a special meeting at Independent Presbyterian Church on May 8, 1874, to air grievances and make a decision on the location once and for all. A large number of Savannahians attended the gathering. General Gilmer seemed irritable and surprised that any public dissatisfaction existed about the chosen location. He offered to tender his resignation, along with those of the other male committee members, if any changes were made. At this point, another highly regarded former Confederate officer, George Anderson Mercer, struck a more conciliatory tone and apparently managed to soothe Gilmer's injured feelings. Mercer reported that former Confederate general Johnston, who was out of town and could not attend the meeting, fully supported the erection of the monument in Forsyth Park. The question was put to a vote, and the Ladies Memorial Association voted unanimously to stick with their plan. The matter was settled.[375]

Just over one month later, the ladies' vision took concrete form as the cornerstone for the monument was laid in Forsyth Park. Before the ceremony, the cornerstone was filled with donations from more than 150 Savannahians. The various and sundry items deposited within included Confederate currency and government bonds whose face value totaled more than $50,000, as well as flags, military buttons, sheet music, Revolutionary War–era currency, rolls and regulation books from local military units, poetry, newspapers, photographs and copies of speeches and important military orders. There was a bronze copy of the Great Seal of the Confederacy, torn bits of flags carried into past battles and a fragment of a flagstaff from Fort Sumter, the scene of the first shots of the war. Savannahians of all classes contributed. A woman referred to simply as "Old Mary," possibly a former slave, contributed one U.S. cent and a $500 Confederate bill. The bric-a-brac revealed a penchant for collecting foreign currency, as coins from eighteen overseas nations went into the container. It seemed as if every attic in the city had been opened and the contents disgorged into the monument.

Shortly after 5:00 p.m. on Tuesday, June 16, 1874, thousands of Savannahians watched as a military parade wound through the streets of Savannah. The *Morning News* reported, "Bull Street presented a perfect panorama of life and beauty, every available location from South Broad to Gaston Street being occupied, whilst on either sidewalk dense throngs hurried along, and the streets were filled with vehicles of every description."

Unlike the earlier procession to Laurel Grove when the Gettysburg remains were laid to rest three years earlier, this march was full of overt references to the Confederacy. Current members of all the city's militia units, including a number of Confederate veterans, marched in uniform. The troops formed three sides of a square around the monument, and members of the Ladies Memorial Association were given seats of honor in the middle. Members of Masonic lodges were heavily represented, and Masonic ritual predominated at the ceremony. After a derrick lifted the cornerstone into place, Masonic officials poured corn, wine and oil onto the stone from silver vessels. Captain Mercer delivered the keynote address, lamenting the passing of "a virtuous Southern life—Alas! Only a beautiful dream of the past." The program culminated with the singing of the Doxology and the firing of eleven cannon blasts—one for each former Confederate state—by the Chatham Artillery. Afterward, participants enjoyed an ice cream festival that helped raise the funds needed to complete the monument. The party lasted until 10:30 p.m., with locomotive headlamps hung high to illuminate the park.[376]

The bulk of the monument's components arrived in Savannah in late December 1874, and by late March of the following year, workers had erected the entire edifice and were awaiting the arrival of the marble statuary and other carved stone pieces.[377] The pomp and pageantry of the cornerstone-laying were repeated on an even grander scale when the city dedicated the memorial on May 24, 1875. The city council passed a resolution requesting all businesses to close their doors at 2:00 p.m. in order to give citizens a chance to participate.[378] The familiar Savannah military parade was rehashed, though this time General Johnston was tapped to be the grand marshal. The great Confederate commander rode on horseback, with other Southern generals, including A.R. Lawton, G. Moxley Sorrel and Henry Rootes Jackson, riding behind. "The streets were literally alive with people," reported the *Morning News*, as the brass bands struck up their tunes and the assemblage set off at precisely 4:00 p.m. The old soldiers found quite a scene on their arrival at Forsyth Park. "The large grounds fairly teemed with animation and life," the *Morning News* proclaimed, "carriages, buggies, horsemen and footmen being jumbled...in almost inextricable confusion." The new monument towered over the crowd, uncovered but entwined with evergreen wreaths. The featured speaker was Savannah's former Confederate congressman, Julian Hartridge, who, in a telling sign of the end of Reconstruction and the return of the prewar power structure, now represented the city in the U.S. Congress. Hartridge delivered his remarks from atop a temporary wooden platform erected level with the top of the six-foot-tall terrace that supported the monument. Once again, the festivities ended with an eleven-gun salute from the Chatham Artillery.[379]

Yet the monument was still incomplete. After spending $21,250—the equivalent of $500,000 in 2016 currency—the Ladies Memorial Association still lacked the additional $5,000 needed to sculpt and place the four soldier statues at the corners of the memorial.[380] Furthermore, Savannahians were apparently none too thrilled with their new monument. Historian and Savannah mayor Thomas Gamble wrote in 1932:

> *When in position the monument proved a distinct disappointment....It was too symbolic to meet popular approval and the general effect was so lacking in charm as to offend those of artistic trend. It was the rococo period in American sculpture and Reid believed in ornamenting every inch of surface in some way....To stand before a monument for a half hour endeavoring to explain what it was intended to convey, struck the average mind as sufficient evidence that the monument was a failure.*[381]

Curiously, all mention of the monument vanishes from the minutes of the Ladies Memorial Association until March 4, 1878, when the following note appears: "A proposition was made by a friend of the Association to remove the figures from the monument, close up the canopy with stone and place a bronze statue of a Confederate Soldier on top. The statue to be given by himself and he also to pay for the stone slabs and the other necessary expense."[382] This was the solution Savannah had been searching for. Yet the ladies took no immediate action in response to this surprising offer, opting to call a special meeting just over two weeks later to take a vote. At this gathering on March 20, the members voted unanimously to accept the proposal. For reasons that are unclear, however, the decision was not made official until the ladies unanimously reaffirmed their decision on April 21.[383]

The benefactor behind this generous offer was fifty-year-old George Wymberly Jones De Renne, descendent of original Georgia colonist Noble Jones and owner of Jones's Wormsloe Plantation. De Renne suffered from a chronic kidney ailment that had prohibited him from serving in the Confederate military during the war. He considered himself a Southern patriot, however, and suffered great personal losses in the conflict, including the destruction of his thirteen-hundred-volume library of priceless books at the hands of Sherman's troops.[384] De Renne revealed his identity to the association in a letter written on April 25, 1878, in which he outlined his goals for the project:

I propose, if this be the purpose of the Association, to place at my own expense on the top of the Column so changed, a Colossal bronze statue of a Confederate Soldier, as he was seen among us—not trim and dapper as a holiday parade; but battle-scarred, weather-beaten, poorly clad and worse shod, perhaps even maimed, with only his weapons in perfect array—a figure of hard service, of veteran experience, of resolute endurance to the end—the type of man who sacrificed all to duty.[385]

De Renne hired Welsh sculptor David Richards of New York to craft the bronze statue, which the artist named simply *Confederate Soldier*. At a time when few monuments in the South depicted actual Confederate soldiers, De Renne and Richards strove to make this figure an accurate representation of how the Southern soldier actually appeared in the field. Prominent local Confederate veteran Captain Hamilton Branch coordinated the effort, assembling and sending to Richards a collection of various uniform parts worn by himself and others during the war. The hat was one Branch wore as a private in the Oglethorpe Light Infantry, when he fought alongside Francis Bartow at the Battle of First Manassas. The coat had been worn by another soldier during the last year of the war. The pants, which were distributed to Georgia soldiers by a relief group late in the war, brought a touch of heightened realism to the ensemble, for, as Branch noted, they were "all scorched out at the ankle by standing too close to the log fires[;] the seat is a great deal worse worn and the [pants] are fastened with a peg instead of a buckle." The rifle in the soldier's hands was Georgia-made as well, at an armory in Athens.[386] In all, judged Branch, the ensemble presented a soldier "as he looked when he marched and fought, and not when he danced and fluted at home."[387] In De Renne's own words, "It represents him as he was."[388]

George Wymberly Jones De Renne was too ill to fight in the war, but afterward, he donated a bronze statue of a Confederate soldier to complete Savannah's monument. *Courtesy of Eudora De Renne Roebling.*

The sculptor and donor paid an equal amount of attention to the figure's posture. Following a suggestion by Captain Branch, the warrior stands in a position known as "parade rest," in which he is still on duty and on the watch for the enemy. De Renne imbued the stance with deep meaning, informing the Ladies Memorial Association in a letter, "It indicates submission to the inevitable, without excluding the idea of manly struggle to avoid it." Also based on a suggestion from Branch, the soldier's hat was pushed back on his head, De Renne explained, so that "winds might cool the heated head and help the man to rest."[389]

The statue arrived in Savannah in April 1879, and it was temporarily exhibited at the joint Oglethorpe Light Infantry/Savannah Cadets armory near Forsyth Park while the association awaited the arrival of the marble slabs required to seal up the niche where "Silence" still stood. The delay was fortuitous, for it gave the ladies and other Savannahians a chance to appreciate up close the many details of the bronze before its installation fifty feet above the park.[390] The sculpture remained at the armory for more than two weeks, with Branch available at specified times to answer visitors' questions in person.[391] Without fanfare or public notice, *Confederate Soldier* was hoisted to the top of the monument in the early morning hours of May 22, 1879.[392] Augustus Schwaab, a German immigrant architect credited with helping to design Savannah's old City Market building in Ellis Square as well as much of the Central of Georgia Railway complex off modern-day Martin Luther King Jr. Drive, was hired to supervise the removal of the marble "Judgement" and "Silence" figures and close up the openings in "Silence's" former perch with solid stone panels.[393] Later, four granite representations of cannon balls were placed on each of the four corners of the monument where designer Robert Reid originally intended statues of Confederate soldiers to stand.[394]

In subsequent decades, controversy arose surrounding the identity of the soldier depicted in De Renne's and Richards's statue. On February 2, 1920, one day after Confederate veteran Major Albert S. Bacon passed away, Bacon's childhood classmate and fellow Confederate veteran Clement Saussy wrote a letter to the editor of the *Savannah Morning News* asserting that Bacon was the model for the statue.[395] Hamilton Branch's daughter Margaret Sexton Branch strongly refuted this claim. Mrs. Sexton confirmed that Bacon was one of several local Confederate veterans pictured in photographs sent to De Renne for his consideration early in the process. Apparently, De Renne thought Bacon looked too suave and sophisticated, so he sent the photo back to Branch, writing on the back, "I want a Confederate Soldier, not a dude." Sexton claimed her father never informed Bacon of De Renne's derogatory comment, nor did he return the picture, out of concern for Bacon's feelings.

Since the bronze would be installed fifty feet above Forsyth Park, De Renne exhibited it for more than two weeks at an armory near the park. *Library of Congress.*

De Renne asked Branch to have photos of himself taken. Branch complied, and it was these two photos, Sexton claimed, that Branch sent to the sculptor. Sexton pointed out that the physique and facial hair of the finished statue more closely resembled her father's than Bacon's. Wrote Sexton:

> *I think if you could see a picture of Mr. Bacon taken in 1878 you will find that he did not wear an "Imperial" but only a mustache and comparing it*

The Confederate Monument as it has appeared since the removal of the marble female figures and installation of the Confederate soldier on May 22, 1879. *Collection of Hugh Golson.*

with the replica [of the statue] *at the Telfair Art Academy no other proof would be necessary that my father and not Mr. Bacon was the man on the monument. It would have been a physical impossibility for Mr. Bacon to wear Papa's uniform.*

Branch was the veteran most associated with the creation of the statue, so it is not surprising that the finished bronze bears a great resemblance to him. As Sexton herself pointed out, however, the sculpture was meant to represent all of Georgia's Confederate veterans—not any specific individual—and so at best, it was, in Sexton's own words, no more than "an idealized likeness of my father."[396]

The twentieth century saw the rise of two popular myths about the Confederate Monument in Forsyth Park: an assertion that no "Yankee" products were used in its creation, and that none of the monument's constituent parts ever touched Northern soil. The earliest printed source for the first misconception appears to be a short human-interest story titled "No Yank Stone Used Here," published in the *Savannah Morning News* on May 7, 1923. Beneath a photo of the monument, the anonymous writer alleges that the Ladies Memorial Association opted to use Canadian sandstone in the base rather than Vermont granite, which was the only domestically available material, because of lingering bitterness about the war.[397] In reality, the Canadian sandstone was part of the package purchased by the association from Montreal-based sculptor Robert Reid, whose family business, Montreal Sculpture and General Marble and Granite Works, provided the materials as well as the design and labor.[398] Georgia granite was readily available to the ladies should they have wanted stone from a former Confederate state, and in fact, that material was used in the creation of contemporaneous Confederate monuments in Macon and Augusta.[399] The claim that none of the monument's components were permitted to pass through former enemy territory seems to have originated in an article Thomas Gamble wrote for the *Savannah Morning News* on April 24, 1932.[400] While the bulk of the materials for the sandstone base of the monument arrived in Savannah aboard the British schooner *Mary Louise* direct from Halifax, Nova Scotia, on Christmas Day 1874, the carved sections, including the two marble figures, were shipped later via New York.[401] In any event, the fact that the statue of a Confederate soldier atop the monument was crafted by a Yankee sculptor and cast in a New York City foundry negates any Confederate propaganda value derived from the memorial's Canadian origins.[402]

The two marble statues installed in the original monument, "Silence" and "Judgement," both found new homes. On May 30, 1879, the association donated "Judgement" to the Thomasville, Georgia Memorial Association. The female figure was erected in the Confederate section of Laurel Hill Cemetery in that south Georgia city, located more than two hundred miles southwest of Savannah, near the Florida border. On

Opposite: "Judgement," photographed in December 2011 in Laurel Hill Cemetery, Thomasville, Georgia. The female figure's trumpet is broken and its bell is missing. *Author's collection.*

Right: Though the inscription on "Silence's" pedestal refers to "the Men of Gettysburg," only one hundred of the soldiers buried in Laurel Grove died in that battle. *Author's collection.*

Below: Today, the marble figure "Silence" presides over more than seven hundred Confederate soldiers' headstones in Laurel Grove Cemetery. *Author's collection.*

the same day that they gifted "Judgement" to Thomasville, the ladies gratefully accepted an offer by local Confederate veteran Captain Henry J. Dickerson "to place at his own expense the statue of Silence on a pedestal over the Gettysburg dead in Laurel Grove Cemetery."[403] Today, "Silence" stands on the eastern edge of Confederate Field atop a marble pedestal inscribed, "To the Confederate Dead. Here rest 'til Roll Call the Men of Gettysburg."[404] Though only one hundred of the approximately seven hundred Confederate soldiers buried here were actually moved from the battlefield at Gettysburg, the inscription on the pedestal has caused many modern-day Savannahians to refer to the entire plot as "Gettysburg Field" and led many to mistakenly believe that most or all of the stones mark the graves of Gettysburg dead.

The Ladies Memorial Association gradually became inactive after the completion of the Confederate Monument in 1879. A core group kept the organization alive primarily to ensure that the memorial and the soldiers' graves in Laurel Grove were well maintained. On June 8, 1897, the association voted itself out of existence and handed over the balance of its treasury to a new organization, the United Daughters of the Confederacy.[405] More than nine decades later, the local chapter of that group returned to the original mission of the Ladies Memorial Association by overhauling and beautifying Confederate Field in Laurel Grove. By the late 1980s, the original circa-1874 headstones placed by the association were in a state of disrepair. Frankie Hodges, a member of the United Daughters of the Confederacy, Savannah Chapter No. 2, began a campaign to replace all 710 markers with new stones provided, surprisingly, by the U.S. Department of Veterans Affairs—part of the same government the soldiers had died fighting to overthrow. Hodges spent two years doing research and collecting the required information on each Confederate soldier. She submitted the paperwork to the authorities and waited months for the new headstones to arrive, scrubbing and cleaning the old headstones in the meantime. Once the first batch of 230-pound granite markers arrived in Savannah, Hodges enlisted the National Guard to move them to the cemetery and a forklift from the *Savannah News-Press* to deliver them to the correct locations. A group of volunteers calling themselves the Confederate Memorial Committee dug holes and set the stones in place. Hodges demonstrated a remarkable ecumenical spirit as she went about the work. "There may be some Yankees out there [in Confederate Field]," she told reporter Derek Smith, "but they will get new headstones. I don't care what flavor they were."[406] While the women who incorporated the Ladies Memorial Association in Savannah in 1868 might have been surprised by Frankie Hodges's forgiving attitude, they would immediately have recognized her determination to do whatever was required to make sure Savannah's fallen soldiers rested with honor and dignity.

NOTES

Chapter 1

1. Williams, *Buildings of Savannah*, 110–11.
2. *Journal of the Public and Secret Proceedings of the Convention of the People of Georgia, Held in Milledgeville and Savannah in 1861, Together with the Ordinances Adopted* (Milledgeville, GA: Broughton, Nisbet, & Barnes, State Printers, 1861), 131, 223.
3. Schott, *Alexander H. Stephens of Georgia*, 20.
4. "Public Meeting," *Savannah Daily Morning News*, March 20, 1861, 2; "Mr. Stephens's Speech," *Savannah Republican*, March 22, 1861, 2; "Vice-President Stephens at the Athenaeum Last Night," *Savannah Daily Morning News*, March 22, 1861, 2; Cleveland, *Alexander H. Stephens*, 717–18.
5. "Mr. Stephens's Speech."
6. "Vice-President Stephens at the Athenaeum Last Night."
7. Cleveland, *Alexander H. Stephens*, 718–21.
8. Ibid., 721–23.
9. Avary, *Recollections of Alexander H. Stephens*, 172.
10. Cleveland, *Alexander H. Stephens*, 741.
11. Avary, *Recollections of Alexander H. Stephens*, 173–74.
12. "Eric," "The Cornerstone of Objectivity."
13. Schott, *Alexander H. Stephens of Georgia*, 519–20.

Chapter 2

14. Kenneth Coleman and Charles Stephen Gurr, eds., *Dictionary of Georgia Biography, Volume One* (Athens: University of Georgia Press, 1983), 64.

15. Francis S. Bartow marriage certificate, Chatham County Probate Court, Savannah, Georgia.

16. Carey Nikonchuk, "Savannah, GA Luxury Historic Homes," Charleston Million Dollar Homes, accessed January 22, 2016, http://charlestonmilliondollarhomes.com/savannah-ga-historic-homes-for-sale.php.

17. Charles J. Johnson, "John Macpherson Berrien (1781–1856)," *New Georgia Encyclopedia*, March 31, 2006, accessed March 16, 2016, http://m.georgiaencyclopedia.org/articles/history-archaeology/john-macpherson-berrien-1781-1856; "John MacPherson Berrien," Ancestry. com, accessed March 16, 2016, http://www.ancestry.com/genealogy/records/john-macpherson-berrien_41137396.

18. *Savannah Daily Morning News*, July 27, 1861, 2.

19. Coleman and Gurr, *Dictionary of Georgia Biography*, 64.

20. *Savannah Daily Morning News*, July 27, 1861, 2.

21. Lee and Agnew, *Historical Record of the City of Savannah*, 107; Henderson, *Oglethorpe Light Infantry*, 2, 9; Rockwell, *Oglethorpe Light Infantry of Savannah*, 4; "Savannah Volunteer Guards Celebrate 200 Years of Service," *Savannah Morning News*, May 5, 2002, accessed October 20, 2016, http://savannahnow.com/stories/050502/LOCkennedyremembers.shtml#.VqvHNbIrJaR; "1st Battalion–118th Field Artillery Regiment, 'Hickory's Howitzers,'" Global Security, accessed October 20, 2016, http://www.globalsecurity.org/military/agency/army/1-118fa.htm.

22. Lilian Bragg, "Francis S. Bartow: A Sketch," in Henderson, *The Oglethorpe Light Infantry*, 4–5.

23. *Savannah Daily Morning News*, July 27, 1861, 2.

24. Ibid., September 27, 1860; clipping in Francis S. Bartow papers, Georgia Historical Society.

25. *Atlanta Daily Intelligencer*, December 29, 1860, in Lawrence, *Present for Mr. Lincoln*, 9.

26. Henderson, *Oglethorpe Light Infantry*, 3, 12.

27. Lawrence, *Present for Mr. Lincoln*, 10.

28. Basinger, *Savannah Volunteer Guards*, 53.

29. Diary of G.A. Mercer (No. 1), April 25, 1861, in Lawrence, *Present for Mr. Lincoln*, 26.

30. Henderson, *Oglethorpe Light Infantry*, 14; Rockwell, *Oglethorpe Light Infantry of Savannah*, 4–5; *Journal of the Congress of the Confederate States of America, 1861–1865*, 1 (Washington, DC: Government Printing Office, 1904), 206. In his letter published on page 1 of the June 26, 1861 issue of the *Savannah Daily Morning News*, Bartow claimed Congressman Louis Wigfall of Texas authored the bill. In the June 11, 1861 issue of the Milledgeville, Georgia *Southern Recorder*, Governor Joseph E. Brown declared, "I consider the act of Congress…a palpable encroachment upon the rights of the States."

31. *Savannah Daily Morning News*, August 1, 1861, 1.

32. Henderson, *Oglethorpe Light Infantry*, 14; Rockwell, *Oglethorpe Light Infantry of Savannah*, 4–5, 10–11.

33. "The Bold Soldier Boy" was played by bands on both sides of the war. It is featured in an illustration of military tunes in the November 23, 1861 issue of *Harper's Weekly* magazine.

34. *Savannah Republican*, May 22, 1861, 2.

35. *Savannah Daily Morning News*, May 22, 1861, 2.

36. Charleston and Savannah Railroad timetable, *Savannah Daily Morning News*, May 20, 1861, 2.

37. *Savannah Republican*, May 22, 1861, 2.

38. *Savannah Daily Morning News*, May 22, 1861, 1.

39. Lawrence, *Present for Mr. Lincoln*, 27–28.

40. *Savannah Daily Morning News*, July 29, 1861, 2.

41. Bartow's message of May 21 and Brown's reply of May 29 were reprinted together in the June 11, 1861 issue of the Milledgeville, Georgia *Southern Recorder*.

42. *Savannah Daily Morning News*, June 26, 1861, 1.

43. *War of the Rebellion: A Compilation of the Official Records of the Union and Confederate Armies* (Washington, DC: U.S. War Department, 1880–1901), ser. 1, 2: 470 (hereinafter cited as OR); "Editorial Correspondence," *Rome (GA) Tri-Weekly Courier*, June 27, 1861, 2.

44. Rockwell, *Oglethorpe Light Infantry of Savannah*, 10–11; Smith, *Civil War Savannah*, 30.

45. Letter from Francis S. Bartow to Frances Lloyd Stebbins, June 23, 1861, in the Francis S. Bartow papers, Georgia Historical Society.

46. "Letter from the Oglethorpes," *Savannah Daily Morning News*, June 6, 1861, 1.

47. "Manassas, First," Civil War Sites Advisory Commission Battle Summary, National Park Service, accessed March 6, 2016, http://www.nps.gov/abpp/battles/va005.htm. The battle narrative in this account is also based on conversations with Lieutenant Colonel Henry W. Persons Jr. and National Park Service historian Jim Burgess of Manassas National Battlefield Park.

48. "The Eighth Georgia Regiment in the Battle at Stone Bridge," *Savannah Daily Morning News*, August 1, 1861, 1.

49. Joslyn, *Charlotte's Boys*, 46.

50. Ibid., 52.

51. "Widespread Interest in Marker to Gen. Francis S. Bartow," *Savannah Morning News*, July 31, 1932, 14; "The Eighth Georgia Regiment in the Battle at Stone Bridge"; "First Battle of Manassas as Compared with Second," *Atlanta Journal*, February 23, 1901. Clipping in collection of Lieutenant Colonel Henry W. Persons Jr.; Lieutenant Colonel Henry W. Persons Jr., e-mail to author, October 25, 2016.

52. *Savannah Daily Morning News*, July 29, 1861, 2.

53. Ibid., August 1, 1861, 1.

54. *Rome (GA) Tri-Weekly Courier*, December 24, 1861, 1.

55. *Savannah Republican*, August 1, 1861, 1.

56. Ibid.

57. *Rome (GA) Weekly Courier*, September 20, 1861, 1. The ceremony began at 2:00 p.m., which organizers asserted was the hour of Bartow's death. In an e-mail from March 9, 2016, National Park Service historian Jim Burgess of Manassas National Battlefield contends Bartow's attack on the Union position likely began around 3:00 p.m., so a time of death between 3:00 p.m. and 4:00 p.m. is more likely.

58. *Savannah Daily Morning News*, July 31, 1861, 1.

59. Joslyn, *Charlotte's Boys*, 45.

60. Ibid., 53, 75,

61. *Rome (GA) Tri-Weekly Courier*, December 24, 1861.

62. Henderson, *Oglethorpe Light Infantry*, 1. The Provisional Confederate Congress closed its second session in Montgomery, Alabama, on May 21, 1861, and convened its third session in Richmond, Virginia, on July 20—the day before the first battle of Manassas.

63. *Savannah Daily Morning News*, July 23, 1861.

64. Ibid., July 29, 1861, 1; *Savannah Daily Morning News*, July 27, 1861, 2; "The Killed and Wounded, *New York Times*, August 1, 1861, accessed October 20, 2016, http://www.nytimes.com/1861/08/01/news/the-killed-and-wounded.html.

65. *Savannah Daily Morning News*, July 27, 1861, 2.

66. *Daily Morning News*, July 26, 1861, 2. Myers, *Children of Pride*, 101. Jones's tenure as mayor of Savannah was October 15, 1860, to October 21, 1861.

67. *Savannah Daily Morning News*, July 29, 1861, 2.

68. Myers, *Children of Pride*, 100–1.

69. Joslyn, *Charlotte's Boys*, 45.

70. *Savannah Daily Morning News*, July 24, 1861, 2.

71. *Rome (GA) Weekly Courier*, September 20, 1861, 1; Joslyn, *Charlotte's Boys*, 53, 75.

72. *Savannah Daily Morning News*, February 3, 1862, 2.

73. Ibid., August 1, 186.

74. Rockwell, *Oglethorpe Light Infantry of Savannah*, 15; Persons Jr., e-mail, October 25, 2016.

75. Legal findings and court actions related to the settling of Bartow's estate are spelled out in documents contained in the Francis S. Bartow file, Chatham County Probate Court.

76. Historic Savannah Foundation president and CEO Daniel C. Carey, e-mail to author, March 18, 2016.

77. "Former Bartow House Bought for Restoration, *Savannah Evening Press*, February 1, 1868. Clipping in the Francis S. Bartow file, Georgia Historical Society.

78. "Antique Dealer Buys Historic Bartow House," *Savannah Morning News*, May 8, 1973. Clipping in the Francis S. Bartow file, Georgia Historical Society.

79. Nikonchuk, "Savannah, GA Luxury Historic Homes."

80. *Rome (GA) Tri-Weekly Courier*, September 14, 1861, 1.

81. *Richmond Daily Dispatch*, September 10, 1861, 1; *Rome (GA) Weekly Courier*, September 20, 1861, 1.

82. "Bartow at Manassas," *Savannah Morning News*, June 2, 1902, 11.

83. *Rome (GA) Tri-Weekly Courier*, December 24, 1861, 1.

84. "What Happened to the 1st Monument–Col. Francis Bartow Monument," Civil War Talk, March 12, 2015, accessed March 7, 2016, http://civilwartalk.com/threads/what-happened-to-the-1st-monument-col-francis-bartow-monument.110613/.

85. "In Honor of Heroes," *Savannah Morning News*, June 3, 1902, 10.

86. "Busts of the Heroes," *Savannah Morning News*, June 1, 1902, 16; "Statues Unveiled," *Savannah Morning News*, June 4, 1862, 12, 6; "Reared by Veterans," *Savannah Morning News*, July 4, 1862, 12; Stewart, *Monuments and Fountains of Savannah*, 383–84.

87. Wiggins, *Georgia's Confederate Monuments*, 19; Henderson, *Roster of the Confederate Soldiers*, 19, 1011.

88. Cope, *On the Swing Shift*, 198, 205.

89. *Housing Authority of Savannah: The History*, 2, in City of Savannah Research Library & Municipal Archives.

90. Jenel Few, "Bartow Elementary Renamed to Honor Otis Brock III," *Savannah Morning News*, October 3, 2013, accessed October 20, 2016, http://savannahnow.com/news/2013-10-02/bartow-elementary-renamed-honor-otis-brock-iii.

Chapter 3

91. Freeman, *R.E. Lee*, 95–6.

92. Ibid., 99–100.

93. Ibid., 101.

94. Smith, *Civil War Savannah*, 46.

95. Freeman, *R.E. Lee*, 102.

96. Ibid.

97. Smith, *Civil War Savannah*, 47–8.

98. Ibid.; OR, ser. 1, 14: 209; Dowdy, *Wartime Papers of R.E. Lee*, 84.

99. Lee, *Recollections and Letters*, 55.

100. Dowdy, *Wartime Papers of R.E. Lee*, 95.

101. Thomas, *Robert E. Lee*, 212.

102. Dowdy, *Wartime Papers of R.E. Lee*, 112.

103. Ibid., 113, 115; "St. Simons Lighthouse History," Coastal Georgia Historical Society, accessed September 22, 2016, http://www.saintsimonslighthouse.org/lhh.html; "Lighthouse History," Tybee Island Light Station and Museum, accessed September 22, 2016, http://www.tybeelighthouse.org/history/history/lighthousehistory.php.

104. Freeman, *R.E. Lee*, 613–14.

105. Ibid., 629.

106. Dowdy, *Wartime Papers of R.E. Lee*, 91, 121–22.

107. Lawrence Martin, "Savannah in the Civil War—A Chronology of Key Events," accessed September 13, 2016, http://www.lakesidepress.com/Savannah-CivilWar/1861-1862.html.

108. Hawes, "Memoirs of Charles H. Olmstead," 63–4.

109. Ibid., 64.

110. Jones Jr., *Siege and Evacuation of Savannah, Georgia*, 7.

111. Mackall, *Son's Recollections of His Father*, 223; Basinger, *Savannah Volunteer Guards*, 92.

112. Jaymi Freiden, "Historic Cannon Recovered off Causton Bluff," *Savannah Morning News*, January 12, 2000, accessed September 15, 2016, http://savannahnow.com/stories/011200/LOCcannon.shtml#.V9rHB_krJaQ; "Cannon That Exploded Near Lee Is Pulled from Wilmington River," Online Athens (*Athens Banner-Herald*), January 13, 2000, accessed September 13, 2016, http://onlineathens.com/stories/011300/new_0113000014.shtml#.V9hJ8vkrJaRat.

113. Dowdy, *Wartime Papers of R.E. Lee*, 122.

114. Freeman, *R.E. Lee*, 628, 78.

115. Smith, *Civil War Savannah*, 46; Mackay family letters, Georgia Historical Society, Savannah, accessed September 15, 2016, http://ghs.galileo.usg.edu/ghs/view?docId=ead/MS%200531-ead.xml;query=;brand=default.

116. "Our Distinguished Guest," *Savannah Daily Morning News*, April 2, 1870, 5; Lee, *Recollections and Letters*, 390, 393; Freeman, *R.E. Lee*, 449–50.

117. Freeman, *R.E. Lee*, 451, 453.

118. Ryan's studio might have been located inside the building occupied today by celebrity chef Paula Deen's Lady & Sons Restaurant. "Savannah Stereoview Collection, MS 018," Jen Library Archives and Special Collections, Savannah College of Art and Design, Savannah, Georgia, accessed October 20, 2016, http://ecollections.scad.edu/iii/cpro/app?id=0603052739583430&itemId=1000235&lang=eng&service=blob&suite=def.

119. "Gen's. R.E. Lee and J.E. Johnston/D.J. Ryan, Savannah, Ga.,"
Library of Congress, accessed September 15, 2016, https://www.loc.
gov/item/2009631003/.

120. Thomas, *Robert E. Lee*, 409.

121. Freeman, *R.E. Lee*, 453.

Chapter 4

122. Scharf, *History of the Confederate States Navy*, 639; Bulloch, *Secret Service of the Confederate States*, 112, 127.

123. "The Arrival at Savannah," *Athens Southern Banner*, November 20, 1861, 2. Edward C. Anderson Diary, November 12, 1861, in Edward Clifford Anderson Papers, Southern Historical Collection, Louis Round Wilson Special Collections Library, University of North Carolina at Chapel Hill.

124. Anderson Diary, November 12, 1861.

125. Scharf, *History of the Confederate States Navy*, 640.

126. *Official Records of the Union and Confederate Navies in the War of the Rebellion* (Washington, DC: War Department, 1894–1922), ser. 1, 12: 324, 380 (hereinafter cited as ORN).

127. ORN, ser. 1, 15: 723.

128. Melton, *Best Station of Them All*, 64–5, 136–38, 146–48.

129. ORN, ser. 1, 14: 273–76; Melton, *Best Station of Them All*, 152.

130. ORN, ser. 1, 14: 273–76.

131. Still, *Iron Afloat*, 129–30; Scales, "Midshipman Dabney Minor Scales Diary," December 14, 1863.

132. Jones, *Life and Services of Commodore Josiah Tattnall*, 224; Still, *Iron Afloat*, 129; Scharf, *History of the Confederate States Navy*, 641.

133. ORN, ser. 1, 14: 275–76; Scales, "Midshipman Dabney Minor Scales Diary," December 3, 1862, April 4, 1863; ORN, ser. 1, 13: 820.

134. "The Capture of the Rebel Iron-Clad Atlanta," *Harper's Weekly*, July 11, 1863, 443: *New York Herald*, August 2, 1862, quoted in *Tri-Weekly Telegraph (Houston, TX)*, September 17, 1862, 1.

135. Gibbes, "Diary of Dr. Robert Reeve Gibbes."

136. Scales, "Midshipman Dabney Minor Scales Diary," January 5, 1863.

137. Melton, *Best Station of Them All*, 185–86.

138. Jones, *Life and Services of Commodore Josiah Tattnall*, 224–25; Scales, "Midshipman Dabney Minor Scales Diary," February 3, 1863.

139. ORN, ser. 1, 13: 767; ORN, ser. 1, 14: 282.

140. ORN, ser. 1, 14: 692; Melton, *Best Station of Them All*, 204.

141. Melton, *Best Station of Them All*, 193–94.

142. "Webbs in History: William Augustine Webb," *Webb Bulletin* 3, issue 1 (January 2012): 1, accessed September 9, 2016, http://www.webbdnaproject.org/resources/WSDP%20WEBB%20BULLETIN%20Vol%203%20Issue%201.pdf; Anderson Diary, 184. This section of the diary has page numbers rather than calendar dates.

143. Melton, *Best Station of Them All*, 217.

144. ORN, ser. 1, 14: 249–51.

145. Ibid., 14: 710–11.

146. Ibid., 14: 263; Still, *Iron Afloat*, 136.

147. ORN, ser. 1, 14: 290; Still, *Iron Afloat*, 136.

148. ORN, ser. 1, 14: 288, 290. Several Northern accounts, including newspaper reports and official U.S. Navy reports, contend the wooden Confederate vessels carried civilian spectators who intended to watch the *Atlanta* capture the monitors; however, no Confederate accounts, including the report of the captain of one of the Southern ships in question, make any such claim.

149. "The Captured Atlanta. Letters from Her Officers and Crew," *Savannah Daily Morning News*, June 27, 1863, 1.

150. ORN, ser. 1, 14: 265.

151. Hunter, *Year on a Monitor*, 75.

152. ORN, ser. 1, 14: 265.

153. "Return of the Atlanta's Crew," *Savannah Daily Morning News*, July 9, 1863, 1.

154. ORN, ser. 1, 14: 290–91.

155. Ibid.

156. Hunter, *Year on a Monitor*, 75–6.

157. ORN, ser. 1, 14: 265, 267, 291; Johnson, *Rear Admiral John Rodgers*, 254; "The Crew of the Atlanta Arrived in Savannah—Their Narrative," *Richmond Daily Dispatch*, July 16, 1863, 1; Melton, *Best Station of Them All*, 228.

158. ORN, ser. 1, 14: 265–66, 291; "The Crew of the Atlanta Arrived in Savannah—Their Narrative"; Davis, *History of the Rebel Steam Ram "Atlanta,"* 7; Johnson, *Rear Admiral John Rodgers*, 254; "The Loss of the Atlanta," *Charleston Daily Courier*, December 29, 1863, 1; "The Capture of the Rebel Iron-Clad 'Atlanta,'" *Harper's Weekly*, July 11, 1863, 443.

159. ORN, ser. 1, 14: 266, 291. "The Loss of the Atlanta."

160. Bulloch, *Secret Service of the Confederate States*, 147.

161. ORN, ser. 1, 14: 265, 291. Melton, *Best Station of Them All*, 229. "The Crew of the Atlanta Arrived in Savannah—Their Narrative."

162. Ibid; "The Captured Atlanta. Letters from Her Officers and Crew"; "News from the Atlanta. She Surrenders Because She Is Disabled. The Crew True to the Last," *Savannah Republican*, June 27, 1863, 1.

163. Davis, *History of the Rebel Steam Ram "Atlanta,"* 7–8.

164. ORN, ser. 1, 14: 289.

165. Johnson, *Rear Admiral John Rodgers*, 256.

166. Hill, *Civil War Sketchbook of Charles Ellery Stedman*, 155.

167. ORN, ser. 1, 14: 267.

168. Hill, *Civil War Sketchbook of Charles Ellery Stedman*, 154; ORN, ser. 1, 14: 265, 287; Johnson, *Rear Admiral John Rodgers*, 255–56.

169. ORN, ser. 1, 14: 267.

170. "The Crew of the Atlanta Arrived in Savannah—Their Narrative."

171. Hill, *Civil War Sketchbook of Charles Ellery Stedman*, 154.

172. "The Loss of the Atlanta"; "The Crew of the Atlanta Arrived in Savannah—Their Narrative"; Johnson, *Rear Admiral John Rodgers*, 256; "NC Civil War Sailors Project," accessed September 12, 2016, http://rblong.net/b-1.html.

173. Hunter, *Year on a Monitor*, 82.

174. Hill, *Civil War Sketchbook of Charles Ellery Stedman*, 154–55.

175. Davis, *History of the Rebel Steam Ram "Atlanta,"* 8.

176. ORN, ser. 1, 14: 266.

177. Scharf, *History of the Confederate States Navy*, 266, 267–68.

178. "Naval Engagement in Warsaw Sound. The Confederate Steamer Atlanta Captured by the Enemy," *Savannah Daily Morning News*, June 18, 1863, 1.

179. *Savannah Daily Morning News*, June 18, 1863, 2.

180. ORN, ser. 1, 14: 288.

181. "News from the Atlanta. She Surrenders Because She Is Disabled."

182. ORN, ser. 1, 14: 291.

183. ORN, ser. 1, 14: 284–5.

184. J.W. Alexander, "How We Escaped from Fort Warren," *New England Magazine* 13, no. 2 (October 1892): 209.

185. "Webbs in History: William Augustine Webb."

186. Hunter, *Year on a Monitor*, 92–3.

187. "Union Volunteer Refreshment Saloon, of Philadelphia," Library of Congress, accessed September 12, 2016, https://www.wdl.org/en/item/9524/.

188. ORN, ser. 1, 14: 277.

189. Hunter, *Year on a Monitor*, 85–6.

190. "USS *Atlanta* (I) ex CSS *Atlanta* (1862–1863), NavSource Online "Old Navy" Ship Photo Archive, accessed September 12, 2016, http://www.navsource.org/archives/09/86/86291.htm.

191. Geden, "Lost Ironclad *Atlanta*."

192. Melton, *Best Station of Them All*, 220.

Chapter 5

193. "Tourism Industry," Savannah Area Chamber of Commerce, accessed October 16, 2016, http://www.savannahchamber.com/economic-development/tourism.

194. *Savannah Daily Morning News*, July 28, 1864, 2; Chris Wilkinson, "Civil War Prisons," New Georgia Encyclopedia, September 9, 2014, accessed October 20, 2016, http://www.georgiaencyclopedia.org/articles/history-archaeology/civil-war-prisons.

195. Andrews, *Footprints of a Regiment*, 147–50.

196. Hadley, *Seven Months a Prisoner*, 78–80.

197. Glazier, *Capture, the Prison Pen, and the Escape*, 132–33; Cosslett, "Reminiscence of Prison Life in the South," 335. The author has been unable to identify any Georgia Confederate officers with this name.

198. Cooper, *In and Out of Rebel Prisons*, 107–08; Abbott, *Prison Life in the South*, 86.

199. Glazier, *Capture, the Prison Pen, and the Escape*, 133.

200. Abbott, *Prison Life in the South*, 90.

201. Ibid., 87; Glazier, *Capture, the Prison Pen, and the Escape*, 135–36.

202. Wilkinson, "Civil War Prisons."

203. Glazier, *Capture, the Prison Pen, and the Escape*, 133.

204. "A Prisoner of War. The Escape of Two Union Officers from Millen, Ga," *Pittson (PA) Gazette*, November 27, 1891, 1.

205. Abbott, *Prison Life in the South*, 423–24.

206. Glazier, *Capture, the Prison Pen, and the Escape*, 133.

207. Cooper, *In and Out of Rebel Prisons*, 107–08.

208. "A Prisoner of War. The Escape of Two Union Officers from Millen, Ga."

209. Glazier, *Capture, the Prison Pen, and the Escape*, 132.

210. Hadley, *Seven Months a Prisoner*, 80–1.

211. "A Prisoner of War. The Escape of Two Union Officers from Millen, Ga."

212. Glazier, *Capture, the Prison Pen, and the Escape*, 134.

213. Cooper, *In and Out of Rebel Prisons*, 114–15.

214. Abbott, *Prison Life in the South*, 90–1.

215. Glazier, *Capture, the Prison Pen, and the Escape*, 135–36.

216. Abbott, *Prison Life in the South*, 90–1.

217. Glazier, *Capture, the Prison Pen, and the Escape*, 136–38. Glazier's story is corroborated in Cosslett, 336.

218. Andrews, *Footprints of a Regiment*, 147–50.

219. Hadley, *Seven Months a Prisoner*, 114.

220. Anderson Diary, September 13, 1864. The date when the Union officers were moved to Charleston is confirmed in Abbot, 101; Andrews, *Footprints of a Regiment*, 147–50; Hadley, *Seven Months a Prisoner*, 81; and Cooper, *In and Out of Rebel Prisons*, 115.

221. Anderson Diary, September 7, 8, 1864.

222. OR, ser. 2, 7: 788–89.

223. Anderson Diary, October 5, 6, 1864.

224. Charles C. Jones Jr. to his mother, September 9, 1864, in Charles Colcock Jones Jr. family papers, Hargrett Rare Book and Manuscript Library.

225. Anderson Diary, September 9, 1864.

226. Ibid., September 8, 9, 1864.

227. Andrews, *Footprints of a Regiment*, 150–53.

228. Ibid.

229. Charles, Kelly and Lankford, *Images from the Storm*, 220–21.

230. Ibid., 222.

231. Schmitt, "Prisoner of War," 90.

232. Anderson Diary, September 9, 1864.

233. Ibid., October 3, 1864.

234. McElroy, *Andersonville*, 421.

235. Kelley, *What I Saw and Suffered in Rebel Prisons*, 72.

236. McElroy, *Andersonville*, 406–07.

237. Anderson Diary, September 11, 18, 1864.

238. McElroy, *Andersonville*, 411.

239. Anderson Diary, September 12, 13, 1864.

240. Ibid., September 15, 1864.

241. Ibid., September 17, 1864.

242. Ibid., October 19, 1864.

243. Ibid., September 25, 1864.

244. Kelley, *What I Saw and Suffered in Rebel Prisons*, 73.

245. Anderson Diary, October 9, 10, 1864.

246. Ibid., October 13, 1864.

247. Andrews, *Footprints of a Regiment*, 147–50.

248. Anderson Diary, October 11, 12, 13, 1864.

249. Ibid., October 18, 1864.

Chapter 6

250. Hughes, "Hardee's Defense of Savannah," 44.

251. "Aid for Savannah. Meeting of the Committee of the Chamber of Commerce," *New York Herald*, January 7, 1865, 1.

252. Hughes, "Hardee's Defense of Savannah," 45.

253. Jones, *Siege and Evacuation of Savannah*, 21; Hughes, "Hardee's Defense of Savannah," 48–51.

254. Jones, *Siege of Savannah*, 78.

255. Jones, *Siege and Evacuation of Savannah*, 111.

256. Henry L. Graves to his mother, December 28, 1864. Graves family papers.

257. Jones, *Siege and Evacuation of Savannah*, 5–6, 74. Sherman, *Memoirs*, 209–10.

258. Jones, *Siege and Evacuation of Savannah*, 22.

259. Blair, *Politician Goes to War*, 217–18; OR, ser. 1, 16: 278.

260. Winther, *With Sherman to the Sea*, 139–40.

261. Berry Benson Papers, 335.

262. Jones, *Siege and Evacuation of Savannah*, 5, 22.

263. Sherman, *Memoirs*, 203; Jones, *Siege and Evacuation of Savannah*, 25–6.

264. Blair, *Politician Goes to War*, 218.

265. Sherman, *Memoirs*, 206, 209–10.

266. OR, ser. 1, 44: 960, 964.

267. Jones, *Siege of Savannah*, 109–10.

268. OR, ser. 1, 44: 962–63; "Rice Fields and Section 106: SHPO Guidance for Federal Agencies and Applicants," South Carolina Department of Archives and History, State Historic Preservation Office, 2011, 4, accessed August 16, 2016, http://shpo.sc.gov/programs/revcomp/Documents/RiceFields.pdf.

269. Jones, *Siege of Savannah*, 134–35; Scaife and Bragg, *Joe Brown's Pets*, 150.

270. Jones, *Siege of Savannah*, 134, 150.

271. Ibid., 148–49; Hughes, "Hardee's Defense of Savannah," 57; OR, ser. 1, 44: 967.

272. "Aid for Savannah. Meeting of the Committee of the Chamber of Commerce."

273. "Google Sunrise and Sunset Time Calculator," accessed 16, 2016, https://www.google.com/?ion=1&espv=2#q=sunset+time+december+20+1864+savannah%2C+ga.

274. Berry Benson Papers, 336.

275. Clark, *Histories of the Several Regiments*, 322.

276. Henry L. Graves to his mother, December 28, 1864.

277. Clark, *Histories of the Several Regiments*, 322.

278. Berry Benson Papers, 337.

279. J.B. Elliott to his mother, January 10, 1865, Habersham-Elliott Papers, Southern Historical Collection, University of North Carolina at Chapel Hill, in Hughes, "Hardee's Defense of Savannah," 58–9.

280. Helen Williams Coxen, "Sixty-Eight Years Since Sherman Visited Savannah," *Savannah Morning News*, December 24, 1932, A5.

281. E.A. Carman, "General Hardee's Escape from Savannah," Military Order of the Loyal Legion of the United States, Commandery of the District of Columbia, War Papers, No. 13, read at the State Meeting of May 3, 1893, 27.

282. *Savannah Republican* editorial, December 21, 1864, in Bruce Mallard, "James Roddy Sneed: There Can Be No Greater Tyranny Than a Muzzled Press," in Patricia G. McNeely, Debra Reddin van Tuyll, and Henry H. Schulte, eds., *Knights of the Quill: Confederate Correspondents and their Civil War Reporting* (West Lafayette IN: Purdue University Press, 2010), 357–58; "Savannah, Interesting Details of the Evacuation and Capture of the City," *Chicago Tribune*, January 7, 1865, 3. ORN, ser. 1, 16: 483.

283. ORN, ser., 1, 16: 279.

284. Carman, "General Hardee's Escape from Savannah," 29.

285. Winther, *With Sherman to the Sea*, 141–42.

286. Ibid., 16.

287. Ibid., 23.

288. Sherman, *Memoirs*, 216–17.

289. Andrews, *Footprints of a Regiment*, 153–56.

290. Coxen, "Sixty-Eight Years Since Sherman Visited Savannah."

291. Michael Turrentine to his sister, December 22, 1864, Michael Turrentine papers.

292. Lovell, *Light of Other Days*, 2–3; Jones, *Siege of Savannah*, 155.

293. Coxen, "Sixty-Eight Years Since Sherman Visited Savannah."

294. Jones, *Siege of Savannah*, 155–56.

295. Coxen, "Sixty-Eight Years Since Sherman Visited Savannah."

296. Nichols, *Story of the Great March*, 96–7.

297. ORN, ser. 1, 16: 279.

298. Gould and Kennedy, *Memoirs of a Dutch Mudsill*.

299. De Haven, "As Wesley Tells It."

300. OR, ser. 1, 16: 280, 310, 319; Lee and Agnew, *Historical Record of the City of Savannah*, 96–7; Lovell, *Light of Other Days*, 2–3.

301. OR, ser. 1, 16: 280; Nichols, *Story of the Great March*, 96.

302. ORN, ser. 1, 16: 481.

303. Robert Watson Civil War Diary, December 20, 1864, typewritten transcript in the archives of the National Civil War Naval Museum, Columbus, Georgia; ORN, ser. 1, 16: 483

304. OR, ser. 1, 16: 280; Watson Diary, December 21, 1864.

305. Watson Diary, December 21, 1864; ORN, ser. 1, 16: 357, 483.

306. "The Siege of Savannah. A Relic of 1864," *Savannah Morning News*, March 9, 182, 3; "Savannah, Interesting Details of the Evacuation and Capture of the City."

307. ORN, ser. 1, 16: 483.

308. John Chipman Gray to his mother, December 25, 1864, in Gray, *War Letters*.

309. Iverson Dutton Graves to his mother, January 20, 1865, Graves family papers.

310. Jones, *Siege of Savannah*, 26; Sherman, *Memoirs*, 217–18; ORN, ser. 1, 16: 800; John Chipman Gray to his mother, December 25, 1864.

311. Carman, "General Hardee's Escape from Savannah," 5; Jones, *Siege of Savannah*, 21.

312. William J. Hardee to Charles C. Jones, May 14, 1866, Charles Colcock Jones papers.

313. Michael Turrentine to his sister, December 22, 1864, Michael Turrentine papers.

Chapter 7

314. Sherman, *Memoirs*, 714.

315. Ibid., 713–14.

316. "From Savannah: Details of the Military Occupation," *New York Times*, January 5, 1865, accessed May 27, 2016, http://www.nytimes.com/1865/01/05/news/savannah-details-military-occupation-judicious-orders-gen-sherman-important.html?pagewanted=all.

317. Lee and Agnew, *Historical Record of the City of Savannah*, 99.

318. Lawrence, *Present for Mr. Lincoln*, 218–19.

319. *Account of the Supplies Sent to Savannah*, 36.

320. Ibid., 35.

321. Lee and Agnew, *Historical Record of the City of Savannah*, 99; "From Savannah: Details of the Military Occupation." The final resolution, pertaining to asking the governor for a statewide vote about whether or not to continue the war, is omitted from Lee and Agnew's *Historical Record* but included in a list of the resolutions printed in the *New York Times*.

322. *Savannah Daily Morning News*, September 27, 1860, Francis S. Bartow papers.

323. "A Journal, Kept by Emma Florence LeConte, from Dec. 31, 1864 to Aug. 6, 1865," January 12, 1865, University of North Carolina at Chapel Hill, accessed May 25, 2016, http://docsouth.unc.edu/fpn/leconteemma/leconte.html.

324. *Augusta Daily Constitutionalist*, March 1, 1865, in Lawrence, *Present for Mr. Lincoln*, 219.

325. *Richmond Times-Dispatch*, January 9, 1865, *Daily Dispatch*, Tufts University, accessed May 25, 2016, http://www.perseus.tufts.edu/hopper/text?doc =Perseus%3atext%3a2006.05.1267.

326. "From Savannah: Details of the Military Occupation."

327. *Account of the Supplies Sent to Savannah*, 21–2.

328. Ibid.

329. "Statement of Elizabeth Georgia Basinger" in Basinger, *"Personal Reminiscences,"* appendix 4; Lawrence, *Present for Mr. Lincoln*, 228; "Elizabeth

Georgia Basinger," Findagrave.com, accessed May 27, 2016, http://image1.findagrave.com/cgi-bin/fg.cgi?page=gr&GRid=70221522.

330. *Frank Leslie's Illustrated Newspaper*, February 25, 1865, 366.

331. "Historical Currency Conversions," accessed May 27, 2016, https://futureboy.us/fsp/dollar.fsp?quantity=56&currency=dollars&fromYear=1865; Sherman, *Memoirs*, 716–17.

332. "From Savannah: Details of the Military Occupation."

Chapter 8

333. "The Savannah Conflagration," *New York Times*, February 3, 1865, accessed July 26, 2016, http://www.nytimes.com/1865/02/03/news/savannah-conflagration-two-destructive-fires-one-night-two-hundred-twenty-five.html.

334. Howard, *In and Out of the Lines*, 200–04.

335. Coffin, *Four Years of Fighting*, 419.

336. "The Fire in Savannah," *Harper's Weekly*, February 18, 1865, 99.

337. Howard, *In and Out of the Lines*, 200–04.

338. Coffin, *Four Years of Fighting*, 419.

339. "Sketches in Savannah, GA," *Frank Leslie's Illustrated Newspaper*, February 25, 1865, 366.

340. "Great Conflagration. A Magazine Destroyed. Terrific Explosion of Shells and Cartridges. Several Blocks Burned. Loss of Life," *Savannah Daily Herald*, January 28, 1865, 2.

341. "Their 60th Anniversary: Mr. and Mrs. H.A. Palmer Married Three Score Years," *Savannah Morning News*, March 10, 1917, 8.

342. "From Savannah: Removing Obstructions in the River. The Recent Fire at Savannah," *New York Times*, February 12, 1865, accessed July 26, 2016, http://www.nytimes.com/1865/02/12/news/from-savannah-removing-obstructions-in-the-river-the-recent-fire-at-savannah.html.

343. *Savannah Daily Loyal Republican*, January 28, 1865, quoted in *New York Times*, February 3, 1865, accessed December 19, 2016, http://www.nytimes.com/1865/02/03/news/savannah-conflagration-two-destructive-fires-one-night-two-hundred-twenty-five.html.

344. "Great Conflagration," 2.

345. Ibid.

346. William Brown Hodgson, "Journal of the Events Connected with Gen'l. Sherman's Capture of Savannah, Jan. 28, 1865," in Charles Colcock Jones Jr. family papers.

347. Lee and Agnew, *Historical Record of the City of Savannah*, 101–02.

Chapter 9

348. "The Graves of Our Confederate Soldiers," *Savannah Daily News &* *Herald*, February 16, 1867, 2.

349. Wheeler, "'Our Confederate Dead,'" 382; "Our Honored Dead. Dedication of the Confederate Monument," *Savannah Morning News*, May 25, 1875, 3; Ed Jackson, "Confederate Memorial Day in Georgia," Galileo: Georgia's Virtual Library, accessed September 28, 2016, http:// georgiainfo.galileo.usg.edu/topics/history/article/modern-georgia-1990-present/confederate-memorial-day-in-georgia.

350. "Decoration of the Graves of the Fallen," *Savannah Daily News and Herald*, April 27, 1863, 3.

351. Torlay, *List of Confederate Soldiers Cemeteries*, 3–16.

352. Minute Book, April 21, 1868, Ladies Memorial Association Records: 1867–1897.

353. Ibid., April 20, 1869; Wheeler, "'Our Confederate Dead,'" 386.

354. Minute Book, May 26, 1869.

355. Ibid., April 19, 1873; Wheeler, "'Our Confederate Dead,'" 386.

356. "Our Honored Dead. Dedication of the Confederate Monument," *Savannah Morning News*.

357. "Going Home: The Exhumation and Re-Burial of the Gettysburg Confederate Dead," *Gettysburg Foundation*, accessed September 27, 2016, http://www.gettysburgfoundation.org/277/going-home-the-exhumation-and-re-burial-of-the-gettysburg-confederate-dead; Thompson, "A (Macabre) Family Affair." The April 20, 1872 entry in the Ladies Memorial Association Minute Book confirms the tally of 101 bodies brought to Savannah from Gettysburg. Since the two groups buried in Confederate Field in Laurel Grove add up to just 100, it is assumed that the 101st body must be buried elsewhere in the cemetery, perhaps in a family plot.

358. "Honor to the Confederate Dead," *Savannah Morning News*, August 22, 1871, 3; "The Confederate Dead," *Savannah Morning News*, September 25, 1871, 3.

359. Minute Book, April 18, 1868.

360. Ibid., April 20, 1869; April 19, 1873; April 20, 1879.

361. Ibid., May 25, 1870.

362. Ibid., February 1873.

363. Stewart, *Monuments and Fountains of Savannah*, 245.

364. Tristin Hopper, "Freshly Defeated in the U.S. Civil War, Confederate Leader Jefferson Davis Came to Canada to Give the Newly Founded Country Defence Tips," *National Post*, July 25, 2014, accessed October 5, 2016, http://news.nationalpost.com/news/canada/freshly-defeated-in-the-u-s-civil-war-confederate-leader-jefferson-davis-came-to-canada-to-give-the-newly-founded-country-defence-tips.

365. "Our Departed Heroes. The Confederate Monument in Savannah. Description of the Beautiful Design," *Savannah Morning News*, August 7, 1873, 3; "The Confederate Monument. The Reasons Why the Park Extensions was Selected for the Location," *Savannah Morning News*, May 7, 1874, 3; "The Confederate Monument. Meeting of the Ladies' Memorial Association," *Savannah Morning News*, May 9, 1874, 3; "Our Honored Dead. Dedication of the Confederate Monument."

366. "Savannah Affairs as Noted by a Correspondent," *Savannah Morning News*, April 30, 1874, 3.

367. "Preparations for Memorial Day," *Savannah Morning News*, April 21, 1873, 3; Stewart, *Monuments and Fountains of Savannah*, 246.

368. "Our Honored Dead. Dedication of the Confederate Monument."

369. "The Confederate Monument. Meeting of the Ladies' Memorial Association."

370. Minute Book, Apr. 19, 1873.

371. "The Confederate Monument. The Reasons Why the Park Extensions was Selected for the Location."

372. Ibid; Minute Book, April 19, 1873, April 13, 1874; "Our Honored Dead. Dedication of the Confederate Monument."

373. "Savannah Affairs as Noted by a Correspondent."

374. "The Confederate Monument. The Reasons Why the Park Extensions was Selected for the Location."

375. "The Confederate Monument. Meeting of the Ladies' Memorial Association"; Minute Book, May 8, 1874.

376. "Laying the Corner Stone. Imposing Military and Civic Demonstration," *Savannah Morning News*, June 17, 1874, 3.

377. "Arrival of the Confederate Monument. An Omission Which Rendered it Liable to Confiscation, *Savannah Morning News*, Dec. 28, 1874, 3; "The Confederate Monument," *Savannah Morning News*, March 26, 1875, 3.

378. Wheeler, "Our Confederate Dead," 391.

379. "Our Honored Dead. Dedication of the Confederate Monument."

380. Ibid; "Historical Currency Conversions."

381. Thomas Gamble, "Material for Confederate Monument was First Subject to Government Confiscation," *Savannah Morning News*, April 24, 1932, Section 3, 1.

382. Minute Book, March 4, 1878.

383. Ibid., March 20, 1878, April 21, 1878.

384. Bragg, *De Renne*, 100–04.

385. George W.J. De Renne to Ladies Memorial Association, April 25, 1878, in Ladies Memorial Association Records: 1878–1879.

386. Bragg, *De Renne*, 139–40.

387. Thomas Gamble, "Figure in Bronze Is No Imagination," *Savannah Morning News*, October 8, 1931, 5.

388. George Wymberley Jones De Renne to the Ladies Memorial Association, Savannah, May 21, 1879, Ladies Memorial Association Records: 1867–1897.

389. George Wymberley Jones De Renne to the Ladies Memorial Association, Savannah, April 28, 1880, Ladies Memorial Association Records: 1867–1897.

390. "The Statue for the Confederate Monument," *Savannah Morning News*, April 25, 1879, 3.

391. "The Confederate Statue," *Savannah Morning News*, May 12, 1897, 3.

392. Bragg, *De Renne*, 141.

393. Account Book, June 26, 1878, Ladies Memorial Association Records: 1867–1897.

394. Minute Book, June 3, 1879.

395. Clement Saussy, letter to the editor, *Savannah Morning News*, February 2, 1920, Savannah Monuments, Tablets, etc. folder, Pamphlet Collection, Kay Cole Genealogy and Local History Room, Bull Street Library, Savannah, GA; "Five Brothers Saussy in the C.S. Army," *Confederate Veteran Magazine*, Dec., 1911, 558.

396. Margaret Branch Sexton to Dr. Wilson, date unknown, accession stamped March 9, 1936, in Savannah Monuments, Tablets, etc. folder.

397. "No Yank Stone Used Here," *Savannah Morning News*, May 7, 1928, Savannah Monuments, Tablets, etc. folder.

398. Wheeler, "Our Confederate Dead," 385.

399. Stewart, 267–68; Gamble, "Material for Confederate Monument."

400. Gamble, "Material for Confederate Monument."

401. "Arrival of the Confederate Monument. An Omission Which Rendered it Liable to Confiscation."

402. Bragg, *De Renne*, 140

403. Minute Book, May 30, 1879.

404. The north panel of the base is inscribed with lines from "Bivouac of the Dead," a poem from the Mexican-American War era by Theodore O'Hara that is quoted in stone in many Civil War cemeteries. The south panel bears lines from "A Soldier's Grave" by Southern poet Eliza P. Nicholson. See Jennie Thornley Clarke, ed., *Songs of the South: Choice Selections from Southern Poets from Colonial Times to the Present Day* (Philadelphia: J.B. Lippincott Company, 1896), 189.

405. Minute Book, June 8, 1897.

406. Derek Smith, "UDC Battles to Keep History Alive," *Savannah Evening Press*, January 20, 1989.

Selected Bibliography

Newspapers

Savannah Historic Newspapers Archive, Digital Library of Georgia. http://savnewspapers.galileo.usg.edu/savnewspapers-j2k/search.

Unpublished Primary Sources

Anderson, Edward C. "Edward C. Anderson Diary, 1861–1862." Edward Clifford Anderson Papers. Southern Historical Collection. Louis Round Wilson Library. University of North Carolina, Chapel Hill.

Basinger, William S. *The Savannah Volunteer Guards, 1858–1882.* Typewritten manuscript. William Starr Basinger Collection. Hargrett Rare Book and Manuscript Library. University of Georgia, Athens.

Basinger, William S., and James G. Basinger. "*Personal Reminiscences* of William Starr Basinger: 1827–1910." GA, J.C. Basinger, 1936.

De Haven, Wesley. "As Wesley Tells It: Excerpts from the Diary and Letters of Wesley W. De Haven, a Soldier in the Union Army, 1863–1865," in "Confederate Letters, Diaries, and Reminiscences 1860–1865," Volume 10, 98. Typewritten transcript in the Georgia State Archives, Morrow, Georgia.

Gibbes, Robert R. "Diary of Dr. Robert Reeve Gibbes, 1861–1865." Typewritten copy in archives, National Civil War Naval Museum. Columbus, Georgia.

Hodgson, William Brown. "Journal of the Events Connected with Gen'l. Sherman's Capture of Savannah, Jan. 28, 1865." Charles Colcock Jones Jr.

family papers. Hargrett Rare Book and Manuscript Library. University of Georgia, Athens.

Scales, Dabney M. "Midshipman Dabney Minor Scales Diary." David M. Rubenstein Rare Book & Manuscript Library. Duke University. Durham, North Carolina.

Archival Collections

Berry Benson Papers. Southern Historical Collection. Louis Round Wilson Special Collections Library. University of North Carolina at Chapel Hill.

Charles Colcock Jones papers. David M. Rubenstein Rare Book & Manuscript Library. Duke University, Durham, North Carolina.

Charles Colcock Jones Jr. family papers. Hargrett Rare Book and Manuscript Library. University of Georgia, Athens.

Charles H. Olmstead Papers, 1860–1865. Southern Historical Collection. Louis Round Wilson Special Collections Library. University of North Carolina at Chapel Hill.

Francis S. Bartow papers. Georgia Historical Society. Savannah, Georgia.

Francis S. Bartow file, Chatham County Probate Court. Savannah, Georgia.

Graves family papers. Stuart A. Rose Manuscript, Archives, & Rare Book Library. Emory University. Atlanta, Georgia.

Ladies Memorial Association records: 1867–1897. Georgia Historical Society. Savannah, Georgia.

Ladies Memorial Association records, 1878–1879. Southern Historical Collection. Louis Round Wilson Special Collections Library. University of North Carolina at Chapel Hill.

Michael Turrentine papers. David M. Rubenstein Rare Book & Manuscript Library. Duke University. Durham, North Carolina.

Savannah Monuments, Tablets, etc. folder. Pamphlet Collection. Kay Cole Genealogy and Local History Room. Bull Street Library. Savannah, Georgia.

Books

Abbott, A.O. *Prison Life in the South During the Years 1864 and 1865.* New York: Harper & Brothers, 1865.

Account of the Supplies Sent to Savannah. Boston: John Wilson and Son, 1865.

Andrews, W.H. *Footprints of a Regiment: A Recollection of the 1ˢᵗ Georgia Regulars 1861–1865.* Atlanta: Longstreet Press, 1992.

Avary, Myrta L. *Recollections of Alexander H. Stephens.* New York: Doubleday, Page & Company, 1910.

Blair, William A., ed. *A Politician Goes to War: The Civil War Letters of John White Geary*. University Park: Pennsylvania State University Press, 1995.

Bragg, William H. *De Renne: Three Generations of a Georgia Family*. Athens: University of Georgia Press, 1999.

Bryan, Charles F., Jr., James C. Kelly, and Nelson D. Lankford, eds. *Images from the Storm: 300 Civil War Images by the Author of* Eye of the Storm. New York: Free Press, 2001.

Bulloch, James D. *The Secret Service of the Confederate States in Europe*. Vol. 1. New York: G.P. Putnam's Sons, 1884.

Clark, Walter, ed. *Histories of the Several Regiments and Battalions from North Carolina in the Great War 1861–'65*. Goldsboro, NC: Nash Brothers, 1901.

Cleveland, Henry. *Alexander H. Stephens, in Public and Private, with Letters and Speeches, Before, During, and Since the War*. Philadelphia: National Publishing Company, 1866.

Coffin, Charles C. *Four Years of Fighting: Personal Observation with the Army and Navy, From the First Battle of Bull Run to the Fall of Richmond*. Boston: Estes and Lauriat, 1885.

Cooper, Alonzo. *In and Out of Rebel Prisons*. Oswego, NY: R.J. Oliphant, 1888.

Cope, Tony. *On the Swing Shift: Building Liberty Ships in Savannah*. Annapolis, MD: Naval Institute Press, 2009.

Cosslett, Charles. "Reminiscence of Prison Life in the South." In *The Story of the 116th Regiment, Pennsylvania Infantry, War of Secession, 1862–1865*, by St. Clair A. Mulholland. Philadelphia: F. McManus, Jr. & Company, 1899.

Davis, Robert S. *History of the Rebel Steam Ram "Atlanta," Now on Exhibition at Foot of Washington Street, For the Benefit of the Union Volunteer Refreshment Saloon, Philadelphia, with an Interesting Account of the Engagement Which Resulted in Her Capture*. Philadelphia: Geo. H. Ives, 1863.

Dowdy, Clifford, ed. *The Wartime Papers of R.E. Lee*. Boston: Little, Brown, 1961.

Freeman, Douglas S. *R.E. Lee: A Biography*. Vol. 1. New York: Charles Scribner's Sons, 1935.

Glazier, Willard W. *The Capture, the Prison Pen, and the Escape*. Hartford, CT: H.E. Goodwin, 1869.

Gould, David, and James B. Kennedy, eds. *Memoirs of a Dutch Mudsill: The "War Memories" of John Henry Otto, Captain, Company D, 21st Regiment Wisconsin Volunteer Infantry*. Kent, OH: Kent State University Press, 2004.

Gray, John C., and John C. Ropes. *War Letters 1862–1865 of John Chipman Gray and John Codman Ropes, with Portraits*. New York: Houghton Mifflin, 1927.

Hadley, John V. *Seven Months a Prisoner*. New York: Charles Scribner's Sons, 1898.

Henderson, Lillian, *Roster of the Confederate Soldiers of Georgia, 1861–1865*. Vol. 2. Hapeville, GA: Longina and Porter, 1959–1964. Accessed March 17, 2016. http://babel.hathitrust.org/cgi/pt?id=wu.89059402289;view=1up;seq=7.

Henderson, Lindsey P., Jr. *The Oglethorpe Light Infantry: A Military History.* Savannah, GA: War Centennial Commission of Savannah and Chatham County, 1961.

Hill, Jim D. *The Civil War Sketchbook of Charles Ellery Stedman, Surgeon, Unites States Navy.* San Rafael, CA: Presidio Press, 1976.

Howard, Frances T. *In and Out of the Lines: An Accurate Account of Incidents During the Occupation of Georgia by Federal Troops in 1864–65.* New York: Neale Publishing Company, 1905.

Hunter, Alvah F. *A Year on a Monitor and the Destruction of Fort Sumter.* Edited by Craig L. Symonds. Columbia: University of South Carolina Press, 1991.

Johnson, Robert E. *Rear Admiral John Rodgers, 1812–1812.* Annapolis, MD: U.S. Naval Institute, 1967.

Jones, Charles C. *The Life and Services of Commodore Josiah Tattnall.* Savannah, GA: Morning News Steam Printing House, 1878.

————. *The Siege and Evacuation of Savannah, Georgia in December 1864. An Address Delivered before the Confederate Survivors' Association, in Augusta, Georgia, on the Occasion of its Twelfth Annual Reunion on Memorial Day, April 26th, 1890.* Augusta, GA: Chronicle Publishing Co., 1890.

————. *The Siege of Savannah in December, 1864, and the Confederate Operations in Georgia and the Third Military District of South Carolina During General Sherman's March from Atlanta to the Sea.* Albany, NY: Joel Munsell, 1874.

Joslyn, Mauriel P., ed. *Charlotte's Boys: Civil War Letters of the Branch Family of Savannah.* Berryville, VA: Rockbridge Publishing Company, 1996.

Kelley, Daniel G. *What I Saw and Suffered in Rebel Prisons.* Buffalo, NY: Matthews & Warren, 1866.

Lawrence, Alexander. *A Present for Mr. Lincoln: The Story of Savannah from Secession to Sherman.* Savannah, GA: Oglethorpe Press, 1997.

Lee, F.D., and J.L. Agnew. *Historical Record of the City of Savannah.* Savannah, GA: J.H. Estill, 1869.

Lee, Robert E., Jr., *Recollections and Letters of General Robert E. Lee.* New York: Doubleday, Page & Company, 1905.

Lovell, Caroline C. *The Light of Other Days.* Macon, GA: Mercer University Press, 1995.

Mackall, William W. *A Son's Recollections of His Father.* New York, E.P. Dutton, 1930.

McElroy, John. *Andersonville: A Story of Rebel Military Prisons.* Toledo, OH: D.R. Locke, 1879.

Melton, Maurice. *The Best Station of Them All: The Savannah Squadron, 1861–1865.* Tuscaloosa: University of Alabama Press, 2012.

Myers, Robert M., ed. *The Children of Pride: Selected Letters of the Family of the Rev. Dr. Charles Colcock Jones from the Years 1860–1868, with the Addition of Several Previously Unpublished Letters.* New Haven, CT: Yale University Press, 1984.

Nichols, George W. *The Story of the Great March from the Diary of a Staff Officer.* New York: Harper & Brothers, 1865.

Rockwell, William S. *The Oglethorpe Light Infantry of Savannah, in Peace and in War: A Brief Sketch of Its Two Companies: A Company, Known in the Confederate States Army as Co. B., 8th Regt. Ga. Vols., and B Company, Known as Co. H., 1st Volunteer Regt. of Ga.* Savannah, GA: J.H. Estill, 1894.

Scaife, William R., and William H. Bragg. *Joe Brown's Pets: The Georgia Militia, 1861–1865.* Macon, GA: Mercer University Press, 2004.

Scharf, J. Thomas. *History of the Confederate States Navy, from Its Organization to the Surrender of Its Last Vessel.* New York: Rogers & Sherwood, 1887.

Schott, Thomas E. *Alexander H. Stephens of Georgia: A Biography.* Baton Rouge: Louisiana State University Press, 1988.

Sherman, William T. *Memoirs of General William T. Sherman, by Himself.* Bloomington: Indiana University Press, 1957.

Smith, Derek. *Civil War Savannah.* Savannah, GA: Frederic C. Beil, 1997.

Still, William N., Jr. *Iron Afloat: The Story of the Confederate Armorclads.* Columbia: University of South Carolina Press, 1985.

Thomas, Emory M. *Robert E Lee: A Biography.* New York: W.W. Norton, 1995.

Torlay, A.F. *List of Confederate Soldiers, Interred in Soldiers' Lots, Laurel Grove Cemetery, and the Catholic and Private Cemeteries, Savannah, Georgia.* Savannah, GA: Morning News Print, 1874.

U.S. Naval War Records Office. *Official Records of the Union and Confederate Navy in the War of the Rebellion.* 30 vols. Washington, DC: Government Printing Office, 1894–1922.

U.S. War Department. *The War of the Rebellion: A Compilation of the Official Records of the Union and Confederate Armies.* 128 vols. Washington, DC: Government Printing Office, 1880–1901.

Wiggins, David N. *Georgia's Confederate Monuments and Cemeteries.* Charleston SC: Arcadia Publishing, 2006.

Williams, Robin B. *Buildings of Savannah.* Charlottesville: University of Virginia Press, 2016.

Winther, Oscar O., ed. *With Sherman to the Sea: The Civil War Letters, Diaries, and Reminiscences of Theodore F. Upson.* Bloomington: Indiana University Press, 1969.

Journals and Newsletters

Geden, Joseph H. "The Lost Ironclad *Atlanta.*" Confederate Naval Historical Society newsletter 54 (July 1990): 4–5.

Hawes, Lilla M., ed. "The Memoirs of Charles H. Olmstead, Part VI." *Georgia Historical Society Quarterly* 44 (March 1960).

Hughes, N.C., Jr. "Hardee's Defense of Savannah." *Georgia Historical Quarterly* 47 (March 1963).

Schmitt, Emil F. "Prisoner of War: Experiences in Southern Prisons." *Wisconsin Magazine of History* 42 (Winter 1958–59): 90–1.

Wheeler, Frank, "'Our Confederate Dead:' The Story Behind Savannah's Confederate Monument." *Georgia Historical Quarterly* 72 (Summer 1998).

Websites

Gettysburg Foundation. "Going Home: The Exhumation and Re-Burial of the Gettysburg Confederate Dead." Accessed September 27, 2016. http://www.gettysburgfoundation.org/277/going-home-the-exhumation-and-re-burial-of-the-gettysburg-confederate-dead.

This Cruel War. "The Cornerstone of Objectivity: Davis' Reaction to Stephens' Speech." August 26, 2015. Accessed July 26, 2016. http://www.thiscruelwar.com/the-cornerstone-of-objectivity/.

Thompson, Kathleen. "A (Macabre) Family Affair: The Weavers and the Gettysburg Dead." *Civil Discourse: A Blog of the Long Civil War Era* (blog). February 8, 2016. Accessed September 27, 2016. http://www.civildiscourse-historyblog.com/blog/2016/2/2/a-macabre-family-affair-the-weavers-and-the-gettysburg-dead.

Academic Papers

Stewart, Dorothy. *The Monuments and Fountains of Savannah.* Department of History. Armstrong College, Savannah, Georgia: 1993.

INDEX

About the Author

M ichael L. Jordan is an accomplished and award-winning filmmaker, television journalist and historian. Michael's travels have taken him around the world to more than forty countries, where he has landed on the decks of aircraft carriers, helmed nuclear submarines, flown combat missions aboard helicopters and patrolled war zones on foot with troops. Michael's extensive film and video portfolio comprises more than a dozen historical documentaries as well as museum orientation films and videos created for archaeologists and historical nonprofits. This is Michael's second book; the first, a coffee table book titled *Savannah Square by Square*, was published by Historic Savannah Foundation in 2015. Michael makes his home in Knoxville, Tennessee, with his wife, Dr. Krista Wiegand, and their son, Joseph. Connect with Michael online at www.michaelljordan.com.